Table of Contents

1. Introduction — 2
2. Chapter One: Defining Goals and Shared Vision — 3
3. Chapter Two: Strategic and Tactical Planning — 26
4. Chapter Three: Building a Culture of Effective Communication — 36
5. Chapter Four: Effective Task Delegation — 46
6. Chapter Five: Continuous Training and Development — 58
7. Chapter Six: Motivation and Accountability — 65
8. Chapter Seven: Continuous Improvement and Innovation — 79
9. Chapter Eight: Adaptation and Response to Changes — 86
10. Chapter Nine: Leadership by Example — 95
11. Chapter Ten: Participation and Collective Decision-Making — 100
12. Chapter Eleven: Developing a Collaborative Work Environment — 112
13. Chapter Twelve: Regular Performance Evaluation — 125
14. Chapter Thirteen: Sustainability and Social Responsibility — 137
15. Chapter Fourteen: Lessons Learned and Future Vision — 145
16. Conclusion — 148

Introduction

In a rapidly changing world, companies and individuals have become the cornerstone of continuous transformation and renewal. Today, each of us lives in a society characterized by dynamism and multiple challenges, necessitating the development of forward-looking visions based on experiences and continuous learning. This book outlines a journey filled with achievements and challenges, interwoven with valuable lessons derived from real-life experiences that highlight the importance of innovation, adaptation, and sustainability in building a prosperous future.

By addressing diverse topics such as effective communication, cultural diversity, and sustainable innovation, this book takes us on an exploratory journey that sheds light on how to overcome challenges and seize opportunities in order to build a brighter and more sustainable future.

Chapter One: Defining Goals and Shared Vision

Identifying the Problem

When Adam took on the role of CEO at "Tech Excel," he began by thoroughly examining the current state of the company. He wanted to understand the reasons behind the company's declining performance and loss of market position. Adam held a series of one-on-one meetings with managers and employees to gather information and understand the challenges they were facing.

Meeting with Leila, the Finance Manager:
In one of the meetings with Leila, Adam discovered significant discrepancies in the budgets allocated to various projects. Leila said, "We have many projects, but there is no clear vision for how to allocate resources. Everyone is working on short-term goals without considering the bigger strategy."

Meeting with Kareem, the Marketing Manager:
During his meeting with Kareem, Adam learned that the marketing teams were working on inconsistent campaigns targeting different markets without clear direction. "Each team thinks they know what's best, but we lack a unified vision to align our efforts. As a result, we are losing focus, and customers do not see a consistent image of our brand," Kareem explained.

Meeting with Sarah, HR Director:
Adam's meeting with Sarah revealed a lack of motivation among employees. Sarah said, "The employees feel frustrated due to the lack of clear goals.

They don't know how their efforts contribute to the overall success of the company. There is a lot of ambiguity and confusion."

Meeting with Youssef, Technology Director:
In his meeting with Youssef, Adam realized that the technology team was working on developing advanced technologies without alignment with current market needs. "We are putting a lot of effort into developing technologies that customers don't currently care about. We need a clear vision to guide our research and development," Youssef explained.

Data Analysis:
After these meetings, Adam asked the analysis team to collect data on the performance of past and current projects. The data showed significant discrepancies in project results, and many had not met their expected goals. It was clear that the company lacked a unified strategic direction.

Initial Meeting
The Knot and Challenges
Adam held a meeting with the leadership team, including the key managers of the company: Sarah, HR Manager; Kareem, Marketing Manager; Leila, Finance Manager; and Youssef, Technology Manager, to share his observations and conclusions.

Adam: "Welcome, everyone. Thank you for coming today. I wanted us to discuss some important issues regarding the company's vision and our shared goals. Let's start with a simple question. What is the current vision of the company?"

Sarah: "I believe our vision is to become the leading company in advanced technology."

Kareem: "Yes, but I see our vision more focused on providing innovative marketing solutions for small and medium-sized businesses."

Leila: "From my perspective, the vision revolves around achieving financial sustainability and sustainable growth."

Youssef: "For me, our vision is to be at the forefront of technological innovation and to deliver high-quality products."

Adam: "I see there is a conflict in the visions. It seems we lack a unified vision. Let's move on to the next question. What are the goals we aim to achieve?"

Sarah: "Our goals are related to enhancing the employee experience and developing their skills."

Kareem: "Our marketing goals are to increase market share by 15% over the next year."

Leila: "Our financial goal is to improve returns on investments and reduce expenses."

Youssef: "We aim to make significant progress in developing our new products and launching them in the market before the end of the year."

Adam: "Again, I notice there is a disparity in the goals. It seems the different teams are striving to achieve different objectives. The last question: How do the efforts of the different teams align to achieve these goals?"

Sarah: "We are working on improving the work environment and offering training programs."

Kareem: "We are focusing on marketing campaigns and strategic partnerships."

Leila: "We are monitoring expenses and looking for new investment opportunities."

Youssef: "We are working on product development and quality improvement."

Adam: "Thank you all for your input. It is clear that we have disparate visions and goals. This conflict confirms to me that the company lacks a unified vision and shared goals. If we want to restore 'Tech Excel' to its market position, we must unite under one vision and shared goals. This is not an option, but a necessity. We need to work together to establish a comprehensive vision that aligns with our goals and strategic directions."

Sarah: "I think we need a dedicated session to define this vision and goals."

Kareem: "I agree with you, Sarah. We need to ensure that all teams are working towards the same objectives."

Leila: "Yes, and this will help us improve coordination between the different departments."

Youssef: "Exactly. If we have a clear vision and shared goals, we will be able to achieve much better results."

Adam: "Then, let's schedule a dedicated working session to focus on defining the company's vision and shared goals. We need to come out with a unified vision and clear goals that all teams can work towards."

Everyone: "Agreed."

Visual Presentation
Adam used a visual presentation to show how a clear vision can lead the team and help achieve success. He showcased examples of successful companies and how a unified vision contributed to their success. He also illustrated the difference between working on scattered projects and working with a unified vision and goals.

Discussion and Challenges
Initially, there were some reservations. Sarah pointed out that employees might feel anxious about the new changes. Kareem added that the market is changing rapidly, and our vision needs to be flexible.

Adam responded, "I understand your concerns, but without clear guidance, we will continue to move aimlessly. We need to be ready to adapt, but we must start somewhere."

> After a long discussion, the team agreed to start developing a shared vision and strategic goals.

Sarah: "I think we need a special session to define this vision and these goals."

Kareem: "I agree with you, Sarah. We need to make sure all teams are working towards the same goals."

Leila: "Yes, and this will help us improve coordination between different departments."

Youssef: "Exactly. If we have a clear vision and shared goals, we will be able to achieve much better results."

Adam: "So, let's schedule a special work session focused on defining the company's vision and shared goals. We need to come out of it with a unified vision and clear goals that all teams can work towards."

Everyone: "Agreed."

Defining the Vision

Work Sessions

Intensive work sessions were organized where all team members participated in setting the vision and goals. The aim was to gather ideas and reach a consensus on the company's future vision. These sessions were interactive and included brainstorming exercises and extensive discussions about the core values important to the company and what the team wants to achieve in the long term.

Adam: "Welcome everyone to these intensive sessions. Our goal today is to set a unified vision and goals for the company. Let's start with a brainstorming exercise. I want each of you to share your vision for the future and the core values you believe are important for the company."

Sarah: "For me, I think one of the core values should be focusing on developing the personal skills and capabilities of our employees. This will help us build a strong and cohesive team."

Kareem: "I agree with you, Sarah. But from my side, I believe innovation should be at the heart of our vision. We need to offer innovative solutions to our clients to stand out in the market."

Leila: "I agree with both of you, but we also need to focus on financial sustainability. We must ensure that all our decisions support sustainable growth and minimize financial risks."

Youssef: "I believe quality is the core value. If we focus on providing high-quality products, we will earn our clients' trust and achieve long-term success."

Adam: "These are great ideas. Now let's talk about the future vision. How do you see the company in five years?"

Sarah: "I see the company as a leader in providing an ideal work environment, where every employee enjoys their work and progresses in their career."

Kareem: "And I see the company at the forefront of technological innovation, with a strong presence in global markets."

Leila: "I aspire for us to be a financially stable company, with a diverse range of products and services that achieve sustainable profits."

Youssef: "And I see us being known for the quality of our products and services, with a broad and loyal customer base."

Adam: "Excellent. Now let's work on integrating these ideas into a unified vision. How can we craft a vision that encompasses all these aspects?"

Sarah: "Maybe we can say: 'Leading innovation in the technology industry and providing solutions that meet and exceed customer expectations.'"

Kareem: "I like that. It's a comprehensive vision that combines innovation, quality, and meeting customer needs."

Leila: "Agreed. And this also indirectly includes the financial aspect, through meeting customer expectations in innovative ways."

Youssef: "I think this is an integrated vision. It includes innovation, quality, professional development, and financial sustainability."

Adam: "Great. We now have a new vision: 'Leading innovation in the technology industry and providing solutions that meet and exceed customer expectations.' This vision will serve as our North Star guiding us into the future. Let's now move on to turning this vision into practical goals."

Sarah: "I suggest we have a goal to improve training and development levels by 20% annually."

Kareem: "And we can set a goal to increase our market share by 15% over the next two years."

Leila: "And I believe we should aim for an annual profit growth rate of at least 10%."

Hala: "In public relations, I think we should aim to improve customer satisfaction by 20% over the next year and enhance the company's overall image through effective public relations campaigns. We should also develop an outstanding customer service system that meets customer expectations quickly and efficiently."

Youssef: "And I would add a goal to improve our product quality, reducing the error rate to less than 2%."

Adam: "These are great goals. Let's start by developing an action plan to achieve these goals. We will define the responsibilities and resources needed for each goal and monitor progress regularly."

Sarah: "This is an excellent start, Adam. I'm excited to work on achieving this vision and these goals."

Kareem: "Me too. Let's get to work and achieve these goals together."

Adam: "Thank you all for your active participation. I'm confident that our collaboration will lead to great success for the company. But we need to share these goals with every team in the company and discuss them to ensure everyone's commitment and motivation."

The New Vision
In the end, they reached a new vision aiming to "Lead innovation in the technology industry and provide solutions that meet customer needs and exceed their expectations." However, Adam and the leadership team didn't just set the goals by themselves; they made sure to involve every team in the company to ensure everyone's commitment and motivation. They held meetings with

each department to discuss the goals and how each team could contribute to achieving them. This active participation increased the sense of responsibility and belonging among employees.

Turning Vision into Practical Goals:

After defining the vision, Adam and his team moved to the next step: turning this vision into achievable strategic goals. This was done through several meetings with each department.

Human Resources Meeting

Adam: "Hello everyone. We're here today to discuss the new vision and goals we've set for the company. I'd like us to talk about how the Human Resources department can contribute to achieving these goals. Sarah, can you start by giving an overview of the vision and goals?"

Sarah: "Sure, Adam. Our vision is 'Leading innovation in the technology industry and providing solutions that meet and exceed customer expectations.' To achieve this vision, we have set several strategic goals, including improving the level of training and development by 20% annually."

Adam: "That's correct. Now, I want to hear from all of you. How do you think the HR department can contribute to achieving this goal?"

Mohammed: "I think we need to develop new training programs focused on innovation and modern technologies. We can bring in external experts to conduct some advanced courses."

Maryam: "Yes, and we can also offer internal training sessions where experienced employees share their knowledge with the team. This will help enhance internal communication and knowledge transfer."

Ali: "I believe we should focus on developing leadership and management skills among new employees. We can design special training programs for potential future leaders."

Sarah: "These are great ideas. Additionally, we can use technology to enhance the training experience, such as using e-learning platforms and online training."

Adam: "I'm happy to hear these innovative ideas. It's important that we ensure all training programs align with the company's vision and support our strategic goals. Sarah, can you coordinate these efforts and develop a clear action plan to achieve this goal?"

Sarah: "Of course, Adam. I'll work with the team to develop an action plan that includes all these ideas and start implementing it immediately."

Adam: "Great. I'd also like us to establish a system to measure our progress and achieve the desired goal. We can set Key Performance Indicators (KPIs) and monitor them regularly."

Mohammed: "We can use periodic reports to measure the effectiveness of training programs and assess improvements in employee performance."

Maryam: "And we can also collect employee feedback on training programs regularly to ensure we meet their needs and expectations."

Adam: "Excellent. So, let's start working on these ideas and ensure the HR department effectively contributes to achieving the company's vision and goals. Thank you all for your enthusiasm and dedication."

Everyone: "Thank you, Adam. We're ready to start."

Finance Department Meeting

Adam: "Hello everyone. Thank you for being here today. As you know, we are working towards achieving our new vision of 'Leading innovation in the technology industry and providing solutions that meet and exceed customer expectations.' To achieve this vision, we have set a series of strategic goals. Leila, can you give an overview of the financial goals we want to achieve?"

Leila: "Certainly, Adam. Among the goals we have set, we aim to achieve an annual profit growth of no less than 10% and ensure strong financial sustainability. We need to focus on improving financial efficiency and better resource management."

Adam: "Great. Now, I would like to hear from all of you. How can the finance department effectively contribute to achieving these goals?"

Ahmed: "I believe we need to enhance our financial analysis processes. We can use advanced analytical tools to better identify opportunities and risks."

Fatima: "Yes, and we can also review operational costs and identify areas where we can reduce expenses without compromising the quality of work."

Khaled: "We can also enhance collaboration between departments to ensure that all financial decisions align with the company's strategic goals. Maybe we can offer training workshops for other departments on budget management and financing."

Leila: "These are good ideas. We can also improve our cash management system to ensure we have sufficient liquidity to face any emergencies. Additionally, we can work on improving the accuracy of our financial forecasts."

Adam: "Excellent. It's very important that we have an integrated financial plan that supports all aspects of our vision. Leila, can you coordinate the efforts and develop an action plan to achieve these goals?"

Leila: "Certainly, Adam. I will work with the team to develop a plan that includes expense analysis, improving financial efficiency, and enhancing cross-departmental collaboration. We will monitor progress regularly and prepare periodic reports."

Ahmed: "We can also develop a system to track financial performance indicators (KPIs) to ensure the goals are being met effectively."

Fatima: "I suggest holding regular meetings to review financial performance and identify any potential challenges early on."

Adam: "Great idea. So, let's start working on these ideas and ensure that the finance department plays a key role in achieving the company's vision. Thank you all for your commitment and dedication."

Everyone: "Thank you, Adam. We are ready to start."

Marketing Department Meeting

Adam: "Hello everyone. I'm glad to see you today. We are here to discuss how the marketing department can contribute to achieving our new vision of 'Leading innovation in the technology industry and providing solutions that meet and exceed customer expectations.' Kareem, can you give an overview of the marketing goals we aim to achieve?"

Kareem: "Of course, Adam. We aim to increase our market share by 15% over the next two years and enhance global brand awareness. We also intend to develop innovative marketing campaigns that attract new customers and retain existing ones."

Adam: "Great. Now, I'd like to hear from all of you. How do you think the marketing department can effectively contribute to achieving these goals?"

Nada: "I believe we can leverage digital marketing more effectively. We can improve our presence on social media platforms and increase audience engagement through distinctive and engaging content."

Omar: "Yes, and we can also develop advertising campaigns targeting new markets. We can use data to analyze customer behavior and identify new growth opportunities."

Maya: "We also see an opportunity in collaborating with digital influencers who can promote our products in innovative ways and reach a wide audience."

Kareem: "These are great ideas. We can also organize online events and webinars to showcase our new technologies and innovative solutions, which will enhance our presence and increase customer interest in our products."

Adam: "Excellent ideas. It's important for us to be creative in our marketing strategies. Kareem, can you coordinate these efforts and develop a detailed action plan to achieve these goals?"

Kareem: "Absolutely, Adam. I will work with the team to develop a comprehensive plan that includes all these ideas. We will focus on improving our marketing campaigns and increasing our engagement with both current and potential customers."

Nada: "We can also provide regular reports to monitor the performance of the campaigns and adjust them as needed to maximize effectiveness."

Omar: "I suggest establishing an internal team to continuously analyze marketing data and provide recommendations to improve performance."

Adam: "Excellent idea, Omar. Let's ensure all our decisions are based on accurate data and in-depth analyses. So, let's start implementing these ideas and ensure that the marketing department plays a key role in achieving our vision. Thank you all for your dedication and creativity."

Everyone: "Thank you, Adam. We are ready to start."

Public Relations and Customer Service Meeting

Adam: "Hello everyone. Thank you for being here today. As you know, we are all working towards achieving our new vision of 'Leading innovation in the technology industry and providing solutions that meet and exceed customer expectations.' Hala, can you give an overview of the goals we aim to achieve in the Public Relations and Customer Service department?"

Hala: "Certainly, Adam. We aim to improve customer satisfaction by 20% over the next year and enhance the company's overall image through effective public relations campaigns. We also aim to develop an outstanding customer service system that meets customer expectations quickly and efficiently."

Adam: "Great. I'd like to hear your ideas on how to achieve these goals. How can the Public Relations and Customer Service department effectively contribute to this?"

Ahmed: "I think we need to improve our communication channels with customers. We can use social media more effectively to interact with customers and respond to their inquiries faster."

Leila: "Yes, and we can also establish an integrated Customer Relationship Management (CRM) system to help us track customer inquiries and resolve their issues more effectively."

Khaled: "We can organize training workshops for the customer service team to enhance their skills in dealing with customers and providing exceptional service."

Hala: "These are great ideas. We can also organize public relations campaigns that focus on our customers' success stories and how our technologies have helped improve their businesses. This will enhance the company's image and increase customer trust."

Adam: "Excellent ideas. It's crucial that we have an integrated system that enhances customer satisfaction and the company's image. Hala, can you coordinate these efforts and develop a detailed action plan to achieve these goals?"

Hala: "Of course, Adam. I will work with the team to develop a comprehensive plan that includes improving communication channels, using CRM, and organizing effective public relations campaigns."

Ahmed: "We can also provide regular reports to monitor customer satisfaction and analyze their feedback to identify areas that need improvement."

Leila: "I suggest conducting regular surveys to measure customer satisfaction and continuously gather their feedback."

Adam: "Great idea, Leila. Let's ensure that we listen to our customers and continuously work to meet their expectations. Let's start implementing these ideas and ensure that the Public Relations and Customer Service department plays a key role in achieving our vision. Thank you all for your commitment and dedication."

Everyone: "Thank you, Adam. We are ready to start."

In this dialogue, it shows how departments can contribute to achieving the company's vision and goals, and the same approach was followed with other departments.

Setting SMART Goals

To effectively implement the vision, Adam ensured that the goals were Specific, Measurable, Achievable, Relevant, and Time-bound (SMART).

The goals were divided into three main categories:
1. Technological Innovation: **Develop innovative products and services that solve real problems and meet market needs.**
2. Market Expansion: **Enter new markets and increase market share in existing ones.**
3. Customer Experience Improvement: **Provide the best customer experience by improving product and service quality and customer support**

Implementation Follow-Up

After defining the vision and goals, Adam and his team began implementing them across the company over the following months. Workshops were organized for all employees to explain the vision and goals and how to achieve them. An executive plan with clear steps to achieve the specified goals was also established.

New Vision, New Success

A goal was set to develop a new product within 12 months, targeting the emerging market and achieving a 90% customer satisfaction rate.

One of the first projects implemented was redesigning the company's website to reflect the new vision and focus on innovation.

The result was a 50% increase in website traffic and a significant improvement in customer interaction with the new products.

After a period of implementing the new vision, Adam and his team faced a significant challenge.
The company's shares suddenly dropped due to the emergence of a strong competitor in the market offering innovative products at competitive prices.
This situation was a dramatic turning point that forced the team to reassess their strategies and quickly adapt to new challenges.

Emergency Meeting

Adam held an emergency meeting with the leadership team to discuss the new crisis. The meeting began with an analytical presentation of the current market situation and the impact of the new competitor on the company's shares. "We have been working hard to achieve our new vision, but the new competitor has turned the tables on us. We need a swift and effective response to maintain our market position," Adam said seriously.

Complex Interaction

Facing this challenge, tension among the managers intensified.
Leila was concerned about the budget and the impact of the new changes on financial resources.
"If we invest in new technologies now, we might risk bankrupting the company.

We need a more conservative strategy," Leila said firmly.

On the other hand, Youssef was enthusiastic about using new technologies to face the competition.
"We must be bold. Innovation is what will attract customers back to us. If we don't move forward now, we'll miss the opportunity," Youssef responded passionately.

Adam's Intervention
Adam noticed that the tension was escalating among the managers and that the disagreement could disrupt the decision-making process. He intervened wisely, emphasizing the importance of unity and working as a team to overcome the crisis.
"We are here not to disagree but to find solutions. We have a vision and goals, and we must be flexible in how we achieve them. Let's combine caution and innovation to move forward step by step."

Periodic Review and Adjustment
The goals and vision were not fixed and unchangeable.
Adam established a system for periodically reviewing the goals so they could be adjusted and updated based on market changes and the competitive environment.
This flexibility helped the company stay ahead and keep up with challenges.

Periodic Review System
Adam and his team decided to meet every three months to review performance and evaluate progress towards achieving the goals. Key Performance Indicators (KPIs)

were used to measure success and identify areas needing improvement.

"We must be ready to change our course if necessary. The market changes quickly, and we need to be flexible and able to adapt to these changes," Adam said in one of the periodic meetings.

Adaptation Results

Thanks to these periodic reviews, the company could quickly adapt to new challenges. For example, some projects were adjusted to align with new market trends, and projects that were no longer viable were canceled. This flexibility and adaptability helped the company regain its balance and grow again.

Through cooperation and teamwork, the team developed new strategies and bridged gaps in the market. The company's shares rose again, proving that "Tech Excel" could adapt and grow even in the toughest conditions.

Lessons Learned:

1. **Importance of a Shared Vision:**
   - Vision is the compass that guides everyone towards the common goal.
   - It contributes to unifying efforts and enhancing team cooperation.
2. **Transforming Vision into Practical Goals:**
   - Goals must be specific and measurable to achieve actual progress.
   - SMART goals ensure clarity and organization in executing the vision.
3. **Effective Participation:**
   - Involving all members in setting goals enhances commitment and motivation.
   - Collaboration and participation increase the sense of belonging and responsibility.
4. **Flexibility in Adjustment:**
   - Goals must be adjustable based on changes in the surrounding environment.
   - Periodic reviews ensure the company stays ahead and capable of adapting to challenges.

Tools and Practical Exercises
Tool: Vision and Goals Card

Develop a Vision and Goals card that each department can use to ensure their efforts align with the company's overall vision.

1. **Vision:** Clarify the company's overall vision.
2. **Strategic Goals:** Identify 3-5 strategic goals.
3. **Key Performance Indicators (KPIs):** Identify indicators to measure progress towards the goals.
4. **Key Activities:** Describe the activities that will help achieve the goals.

Exercise: Brainstorming Session

Gather your team for a brainstorming session to define the vision and goals for your department. Use the following questions as a guide:

- What is the company's strategic direction?
- What goals need to be achieved to realize this vision?
- How can we measure progress?

Inspirational Quotes

"Vision is not just a picture of what could be; it is an appeal to our better selves, a call to become something more." - Jonathan Swift

"Goals are not dreams; they are plans with a deadline." - Harvey Mackay

---

Discussion Questions

1. How can a clear vision impact team performance?
2. What challenges might arise when trying to establish a shared vision?
3. How can we ensure all team members are committed to the shared vision and goals?

Chapter Two: Strategic and Tactical Planning

After Adam and his team defined the shared vision and goals, the next step was to develop a clear strategic and tactical plan to achieve these goals. Adam realized that success cannot be achieved without a well-thought-out and integrated plan to guide the company towards its vision.

Strategic Planning Meeting

Adam held an extensive meeting with the leadership team to discuss strategic and tactical plans. All key managers attended the meeting: Sarah, Kareem, Leila, Youssef, Hala, along with some key employees from various departments.

"Now that we've defined our vision and goals, we need to lay out a clear strategic plan to get there. This plan will be our roadmap to achieving success," Adam began the meeting.

Current Situation Analysis

SWOT Analysis

The meeting started with a SWOT analysis session (Strengths, Weaknesses, Opportunities, Threats).

Kareem led this session, where the team identified and assessed internal and external factors that could affect the company.

- **Strengths:** Team's expertise in technology, good company reputation.

- **Weaknesses:** Lack of financial resources, absence of certain skills.
- **Opportunities:** Market expansion, increased demand for modern technology.
- **Threats:** Emergence of new competitors, market fluctuations.

"This analysis will help us better understand our position and how to leverage our strengths and overcome our weaknesses," Kareem explained.

Setting Strategic Goals
Defining Strategic Goals
After the SWOT analysis, the team identified the main strategic goals that would guide the company over the next three years.

The goals were based on the new vision and market needs.

- **Innovation:** Develop new technologies and products that meet customer needs.
- **Expansion:** Enter new markets and increase market share.
- **Efficiency:** Improve internal processes and increase productivity.
- **Development:** Invest in employee training and development.

"We need to be ambitious but realistic at the same time. These goals will lead us to achieve our vision," Adam emphasized the importance of balancing ambition with realism.

Tactical Planning

Tactical Planning

After defining the strategic goals, the teams began to create short-term tactical plans to achieve these initiatives. They used a breakdown approach to transform large goals into smaller, more detailed steps that could be executed within specific time frames.

Technology Team

Youssef: "Alright, we have a big goal of improving our technology platform to meet the increasing needs of our customers. Let's break this goal down into smaller steps. What do you suggest for the first phase?"

Sarah (Software Engineer): "I think we should start by analyzing feedback and comments from current customers to identify areas that need improvement. This can be the basis for setting development priorities."

Ali (Project Manager): "Excellent. We can use data analysis tools to gather this information and create a comprehensive report. Then, we can break the work down into smaller teams to develop each new feature separately."

Youssef: "I agree with you. Let's start collecting and analyzing data during the first week, then dedicate the following two weeks to developing the most requested features."

Marketing Team

Kareem: "We need to increase our market share by 15% over the next two years. How can we turn this big goal into actionable steps?"

Nada (Digital Marketing Manager): "We can start a comprehensive marketing campaign on social media targeting new markets. We should break this campaign into phases starting with awareness, then engagement, and finally conversion."

Omar (Marketing Analyst): "I also suggest leveraging marketing analytics to precisely identify the target audience and direct ads to them effectively."

Kareem: "Excellent. Let's start with the first phase of the campaign, which is the awareness phase. We'll dedicate the first month to creating attractive content and posting it across all social channels. After that, we'll move to the engagement phase."

Finance Team

Leila: "Our goal is to improve financial efficiency and better manage resources. How can we break this down into actionable steps?"

Ahmed (Accountant): "We can start by reviewing and analyzing current expenses to identify areas where we can reduce costs without affecting the quality of work."

Fatima (Financial Analysis Manager): "Yes, and we can also develop a system to monitor financial performance regularly and provide monthly reports that allow us to track progress and achieve financial goals."

Leila: "Great. Let's dedicate the next two weeks to reviewing and analyzing expenses, then start setting up the monitoring system and providing monthly reports."

Customer Service Team

Hala: "Our goal is to improve customer satisfaction by 20%. How can we achieve this through specific steps?"

Khaled (Customer Service Representative): "We can start by improving the Customer Relationship Management (CRM) system to track all customer inquiries and resolve their issues faster."

Maya (Training Manager): "Also, we can organize training workshops for the customer service team to improve their skills in dealing with customers and providing excellent service."

Hala: "Excellent idea. Let's start by updating the CRM system in the first month, then organize the training workshops in the following month."

In this way, the teams break down large strategic goals into small, actionable tactical steps, helping them achieve their objectives in an organized and efficient manner over specified time periods.

Yusuf led the tactical planning session for the technology team:
- Developing a roadmap for new technologies, prioritizing research and development.

Leila led the planning session for the finance team:
- Creating a detailed budget for new projects, determining the required financial resources.

Kareem led the planning session for the marketing team:
- Designing marketing campaigns targeting new markets, enhancing the brand.

Sarah led the planning session for the HR team:
- Developing new training programs, improving recruitment strategies.

"Tactical planning is how we achieve our strategic goals. Each team must know its role and strive to achieve it efficiently," said Adam.

Resource Management and Allocation
A critical aspect of tactical planning was effective resource allocation. Adam ensured that all teams had the necessary resources (financial, human, technical) to implement their plans. He reviewed and distributed budgets according to priorities.

Setting Timelines and Assigning Responsibilities
Adam and his team set clear timelines for each step of the tactical plans, assigning responsibilities to each team member. They used project management tools to track progress and ensure deadlines were met.

- Project management tools are programs and software that help teams and companies plan, execute, and track progress on projects. These tools provide a way to organize work, improve communication, and ensure deadlines are met. Some of the most notable project management tools include:
  - Trello
  - Asana
  - Jira
  - Microsoft Project
  - Basecamp
  - Smartsheet
  - Redmine
  - Clarizen
  - Monday.com
  - Wrike

The technology team at "Tech Excel" used one of these programs to organize a new product development project. They created a plan that included all tasks such as research, development, testing, and launch. Tasks were distributed to team members with set deadlines for each task.

- **Research:** Gather information and analyze the market.
- **Development:** Build the product prototype.
- **Testing:** Test the prototype and ensure quality.
- **Launch:** Prepare the marketing campaign and launch the product.

Using the program, the team was able to easily track progress, collaborate effectively, and ensure deadlines were met.

Implementation and Follow-up

The teams began implementing the tactical plans. Adam established a periodic follow-up system to ensure progress and goal achievement.

- **Monthly follow-up meetings:** To review progress, solve problems, and adjust plans as needed.
- **Regular performance reports:** To evaluate goal achievement and key performance indicators (KPIs).
- **Semi-annual evaluation sessions:** To assess overall performance and identify successes and challenges.

Adapting to Changes

"Good implementation requires continuous follow-up and constant adjustments. We cannot succeed if we are not flexible and able to adapt," Adam said in one of the follow-up meetings.
The ability to adapt to changes was an essential part of tactical planning.
Adam understood that the dynamic market required flexibility in planning and execution.
Therefore, there was a system in place to regularly review and adjust plans based on market and technology changes.

With these steps, the technology team was able to develop a new product with innovative technology, which increased customer loyalty and generated significant sales.
Meanwhile, the marketing team succeeded in entering a new market, leading to a 20% increase in the company's market share.

Adam and his team managed to establish a strong strategic and tactical plan, which helped "Tech Excel" move forward confidently towards achieving its vision and goals.

Lessons Learned:

1. **Strategic Planning Turns Vision into Reality:**
   - Strategic planning helps turn big goals into achievable initiatives.
   - SWOT analysis helps in understanding the current situation and identifying appropriate strategies.
2. **Tactical Planning Ensures Effective Execution:**
   - Tactical plans turn big goals into actionable steps.
   - Setting clear timelines and distributing responsibilities ensures organized commitment and execution.
3. **Efficient Resource Management:**
   - Effective resource allocation ensures teams have what they need to achieve goals.
   - Reviewing budgets and prioritizing allocations enhances execution effectiveness.
4. **Regular Follow-up and Adaptation to Changes:**
   - Regular follow-up meetings help maintain momentum.
   - The ability to adapt to changes ensures continuous success and avoids failure.

Practical Tools and Exercises
Tool: Strategic Plan Template

1. Vision: Describe the company's overall vision.
2. Strategic Goals: Identify 3-5 key strategic goals.
3. Internal and External Analysis: Use SWOT analysis.
4. Tactical Plans: Develop plans for each team to achieve the goals.
5. Performance Indicators: Determine KPIs to track progress.

Exercise: Strategic Planning Workshop

Gather your team in a workshop to identify strategic goals and develop tactical plans. Use SWOT analysis as a starting point, then create detailed plans for each team.

Inspirational Quotes

"Planning is not the end of thinking, but the beginning." - Blanchard and Hagler

"Strategy is about making choices that create a unique position." - Michael Porter

---

Discussion Questions

1. What is the importance of strategic planning in achieving goals?
2. How can SWOT analysis be used to identify effective strategies?
3. What challenges might be faced in the tactical planning process, and how can they be overcome?

Chapter Three: Building an Effective Communication Culture

After setting the vision, common goals, and strategic and tactical plans, Adam realized that the success of "Tech Excel" heavily depended on effective communication among team members.
It was clear that there were communication gaps between different teams within the company, leading to misunderstandings and project delays.

Discovering Communication Gaps
The story began when Adam received reports from department managers about unexplained project delays and discrepancies in goal understanding among different teams. Adam decided to hold individual meetings with each department to uncover the source of the problem. Through these meetings, he discovered that the lack of effective communication was the main cause of many issues.
Therefore, he focused on building a transparent and open communication culture.

The Importance of Effective Communication
Evaluating the Current Situation
Adam held a workshop involving all employees to assess the current state of communication within the company. He asked employees to share their experiences and examples of misunderstandings or delays resulting from poor communication. Some of the issues included:
1- Misunderstanding Project Requirements
   In a major project to develop a new application, there was a misunderstanding between the development team and the marketing team regarding the final

requirements for the application. The marketing team expected some additional features that were not clearly communicated to the development team.
- Case: The marketing team requested the addition of a specific feature in the application. The request was sent via a short and vague email without sufficient details.
- Result: The development team misunderstood the request and started developing a completely different feature.
- Impact: The teams discovered the problem after several weeks, leading to a significant project delay and increased costs due to the wasted time on developing the wrong feature.

2- Delays in Task Execution Due to Poor Communication

In another project, there was a delay in executing critical tasks due to poor communication between the project management team and the technical support team.
- Case: The project management team was waiting for the technical support team to set up the necessary infrastructure to start work on certain tasks. The request was communicated verbally only and was not documented or properly followed up.
- Result: The technical support team was not aware of the high priority of the required tasks and focused on less important tasks.
- Impact: As a result, the critical tasks were delayed by a few weeks, leading to a delay in the overall project timeline.

Impacts of Poor Communication
- Schedule Delays: Misunderstandings and poor communication lead to significant delays in project execution.
- Increased Costs: Rework and correcting errors due to misunderstandings lead to increased costs.
- Low Morale: Poor communication and misunderstandings lead to team frustration and low employee morale.

How to Handle These Situations
- Document Requirements: Clearly and thoroughly document all requirements and expectations to ensure all parties understand.
- Regular Meetings: Hold regular meetings to review progress and ensure everyone is on the same page.
- Set Priorities: Clearly define priorities and identify critical tasks to ensure focus.

With these examples, the team can understand the importance of effective communication and avoid issues caused by misunderstandings or delays.

Through this workshop, the team gained a deep understanding of the problems everyone faces.

Adam began by emphasizing the importance of effective communication in achieving common goals. Adam said in a leadership team meeting, "Without effective communication, we cannot achieve our goals. Good communication enhances understanding, builds trust, and helps us work as one team."

Based on their findings, Adam developed a comprehensive strategy to improve communication.

The strategy focused on three main areas:
1. **Internal Communication:**
   - Encourage weekly team meetings to discuss progress and potential issues.
   - Use digital communication tools like project management applications and instant messaging apps to facilitate daily communication.
2. **Interdepartmental Communication:**
   - Organize monthly meetings bringing together representatives from all departments to discuss joint projects and challenges.
   - Create joint working committees with members from various departments to work on major projects.
3. **Communication with Upper Management:**
   - Hold quarterly meetings with upper management to review progress and strategic issues.
   - Establish a direct communication channel with the CEO for questions and ideas.

Communication Tools
Choosing the Right Communication Tools
Adam and his team decided to use a set of communication tools to ensure smooth information flow among all team members. The tools included:
- Project management applications like Asana or Trello to organize tasks and track progress.
- Instant messaging applications like Slack to enhance fast and direct communication.
- Virtual meeting tools like Zoom to facilitate communication among remote teams.

"We need to choose tools that fit our needs and ensure effective communication," said Youssef, the technology manager.

Rules for Effective Communication

Establishing Rules for Effective Communication

Adam realized that improving tools and structures is not enough without enhancing employees' communication skills. So, he organized a series of training sessions focusing on:

- Active listening skills: **Teaching employees how to listen attentively and understand others' problems and needs.**
- Clear speaking skills: **Training employees to express their ideas clearly and use simple, direct language.**
- Conflict resolution skills: **Providing techniques to manage conflicts constructively and avoid escalation.**

"Communication is not just about talking, but also about listening. We need to be good listeners to understand our team's issues and needs," Adam emphasized.

He then established some basic rules for effective communication to ensure communication in the company is consistent and clear:

- Clarity: **Messages should be clear and direct.**
- Transparency: **Information should be shared honestly and without concealment.**
- Timeliness: **Messages should be timely to avoid work delays.**
- Active listening: **Everyone should listen attentively and provide constructive feedback.**

Regular Communication Sessions

Holding Regular Communication Sessions

To enhance effective communication, Adam decided to hold regular communication sessions with the team. These sessions included:

- Weekly meetings: **To review progress and discuss any challenges or issues.**

- One-on-one meetings: **Between managers and employees to discuss performance and provide guidance.**
- Communication workshops: **To improve communication skills among team members.**

"We need to make communication a part of our daily culture, not just something we do when problems arise," Adam said in one of the meetings.

After a period of improving communication, the company faced a major challenge. There was a defect in one of the products that led to customer dissatisfaction and an increase in complaints. This situation was a real test of the team's communication effectiveness.

Complex Interaction

During the crisis, there was a divergence of opinions among the managers on how to handle the issue.

Adam: "Hello everyone. As you know, we are facing a major challenge due to a defect in one of our products and an increase in customer complaints. This crisis is a real test of our internal communication and customer service effectiveness. Hala, how do we address this situation from a public relations and customer service perspective?"

Hala: "We need to be transparent and quick in our response. We should issue an official statement explaining the problem and apologizing to the affected customers. Additionally, we should plan appropriate compensation for the customers."

Leila: "I agree with you, Hala. We need to show customers that we care about their problems and appreciate their patience."

Youssef: "But we also need to ensure that we work on resolving the technical issue quickly and effectively so that it doesn't happen again."

Adam: "Yes, Youssef. We need to combine both approaches. Hala, how can we implement this in an integrated manner?"

Hala: "I suggest we start by issuing an official statement that explains the problem and offers a sincere apology. Then, we will begin contacting the affected customers individually to inform them of the actions we are taking to resolve the issue and compensate them."

Maya (Training Manager): "We can also organize training workshops for the customer service team to improve their skills in handling complaints and managing crises."

Khalid (Customer Service Representative): "Additionally, we can create a database to track all complaints and ensure that each case is followed up until it is fully resolved."

Adam: "Good idea, Khalid. Let's ensure that the customer service team is fully equipped to handle this crisis efficiently. Can we prepare a detailed action plan that includes these steps?"

Hala: "Yes, I will work with the team to create a plan that includes issuing the official statement, contacting the affected customers, and training the team on crisis management."

Leila: "And I will work on determining the budget needed to compensate the customers and ensure that we have sufficient financial resources to handle this crisis."

Youssef: "And I will oversee the technical team to ensure the issue is resolved quickly and effectively and to prevent it from happening again in the future."

Adam: "Thank you all. Remember, effective communication and collaboration are what will get us through this crisis stronger. Let's start implementing this plan immediately."

Everyone: "Ready, Adam."

After improving the communication culture, the team noticed a significant improvement in teamwork and an increase in employee productivity.

For example:
- **New product development project:** Thanks to effective communication, the project was completed ahead of schedule with high quality.
- **Customer service improvement:** Thanks to transparency and good communication, the number of complaints was reduced and customer satisfaction increased.

Lessons learned:

1. **The importance of effective communication:**
   - Effective communication is the backbone of any successful organization.
   - Poor communication leads to misunderstandings and delays in project execution.
2. **Internal communication:**
   - Regular meetings and digital communication tools enhance collaboration and understanding among team members.
   - Active listening and clear speaking are essential skills for improving communication.
3. **Inter-departmental communication:**
   - Joint meetings and working committees enhance understanding and cooperation between different departments.
   - Opening direct communication channels with senior management enhances transparency and trust.
4. **Training and communication tools:**
   - Training in communication skills contributes to improving team performance.
   - Using effective communication tools facilitates project management and daily communication.

Tools and Practical Exercises
Tool: Effective Communication Plan Template
1. Setting Goals: What are the main goals for team communication?
2. Choosing Tools: What tools will be used for communication?
3. Establishing Rules: What rules will guide team communication?
4. Regular Evaluation: How will the effectiveness of communication be assessed and improved?

Exercise: Workshop to Improve Communication Skills
Gather your team for a workshop to enhance communication skills. Provide short lectures on active listening, transparency, and giving constructive feedback. Then, divide the team into small groups to practice these skills through real-life scenarios.

Inspiring Quotes
"Communication is the lifeline of any successful team." - John C. Maxwell

"The best way to overcome difficulties is to talk about them openly." - Dale Carnegie

---

Discussion Questions
1. How can the communication culture in your team be improved?
2. What are the most effective tools to facilitate communication at work?
3. How can conflicts within the team be handled constructively?

Chapter Four: Delegating Tasks Effectively

Delegating tasks is one of the essential elements for achieving success in any organization.
After Adam and his team worked on improving communication, the next challenge was to enhance work efficiency through proper task delegation.
Adam discovered that some managers were hesitant to delegate tasks due to fear of losing control or lack of trust in the team's ability to execute tasks correctly. This issue led to manager burnout and project delays. He noticed that managers were spending too much time on operational tasks, hindering their ability to focus on strategic planning. He held a meeting with the leadership team to discuss this problem. During the meeting, it became clear that there was significant hesitation in delegating tasks, and managers felt pressured due to the excessive operational workload. Thus, they realized the need to improve their task delegation skills to ensure efficient work execution and the importance of this in enhancing productivity and employee development.

The Importance of Delegating Tasks

Adam: "Welcome everyone. Today we want to talk about the task delegation process and the importance of appropriately distributing the workload. I've noticed some hesitation in delegating tasks. Can you share how you feel about this topic?"

Leila: "Honestly, Adam, I feel anxious when I delegate some critical tasks. I'm worried about the quality being affected or the work being delayed."

Youssef: "I feel the same. We work on sensitive technical projects, and sometimes I think it's easier and safer to do the tasks myself rather than risk delegating them."

Adam: "I understand your concerns completely. But this added pressure on managers can be harmful. We need to find a way to alleviate these burdens. Leila, do you think there's something we can do to increase your confidence in delegating tasks?"

Leila: "Maybe if we had a training program to develop employees' skills, I would feel more comfortable delegating tasks."

Adam: "That's a good suggestion. Yusuf, what about you? How can we help you feel confident in delegating tasks?"

Youssef: "I think improving the follow-up system would be beneficial. If we had a clear mechanism to track progress and ensure everything is going according to plan, I might feel more comfortable delegating tasks."

Adam: "Great idea. We will work on improving the follow-up system and providing the necessary support. Our goal is to build greater trust between managers and employees. Delegating tasks is not just about offloading burdens to free up managers' time; it's also a way to develop employees' skills and build trust within the team. It's also an opportunity to develop our team and make it more efficient."

Leila: "Yes, I think that could be helpful. If employees are well-trained and properly monitored, it can help reduce the pressure."

Youssef: "Exactly. And I think regularly providing constructive feedback can also help improve performance and increase confidence."

Adam: "So, we'll start by setting up a comprehensive training program to improve employees' skills, and we'll establish an effective follow-up system. Our goal is to empower every team member to perform their tasks efficiently, allowing us all to focus on strategic aspects instead of getting bogged down in operational details."

Sarah: "Excellent, Adam. I feel this will be a big step towards improving our teamwork and reducing the burden on managers."

Hala: "I agree with you, Sarah. Let's start implementing these ideas as soon as possible."

Adam: "Thank you all for your honesty. Let's work together to achieve these goals and make the task delegation process more effective and successful."

Therefore, they realized that they needed to improve their task delegation skills effectively to ensure efficient execution of work. The importance of this lies in boosting productivity and developing employees.

Adam decided to organize a workshop on task delegation. With the leadership team and several employees present, the workshop began with a presentation on the importance of delegation in improving productivity and empowering the team.

Adam explained how proper delegation can enhance the team's capabilities and lighten the load on managers.

Adam: "Welcome everyone to the task delegation workshop. Today's goal is to discuss the importance of delegation and how we can improve this process in our company. Proper delegation is not just a way to distribute burdens, but also a tool to empower the team and increase productivity."

(The presentation begins)

Adam: "First, let's talk about the benefits of delegation. When delegation is done correctly, managers can focus on strategic goals instead of getting bogged down in daily tasks. This can increase work efficiency and contribute to developing employees' leadership skills."

(Displays a slide showing statistics and benefits)

Adam: "According to studies, companies that rely on effective delegation achieve 30% higher productivity and have greater flexibility in dealing with challenges. Let's hear from you, what difficulties do you face when delegating tasks?"

Leila: "For me, I find it challenging to ensure that the task will be done with the same quality I expect if I don't do it myself."

Youssef: "I share Leila's concern. In technology projects, any small mistake can be costly. So, I tend to execute the tasks myself to ensure quality."

Adam: "That's understandable. But remember, proper delegation involves training employees and providing them with the necessary resources and support. Let's talk about the steps of effective delegation."

(Displays a slide containing the steps of effective delegation)

Adam: "First, choosing the right person. It's important to know the strengths and weaknesses of each team member. Second, clearly defining expectations. Third, providing the necessary support and resources. And finally, tracking progress and providing regular feedback."

Kareem: "So, how do we choose the right person?"

Adam: "Good question. Let's talk about identifying strengths and weaknesses. Let's start with a simple exercise. Each manager writes a list of strengths and weaknesses for each member of their team."

(The managers start writing the lists)

Leila: "Adam, I think this exercise will help us a lot. There are members of my team who have certain skills that I hadn't noticed."

Adam: "Exactly, Leila. The goal is to recognize the potential of each team member. Now, let's move on to clarifying expectations."

(Displays a slide on how to clarify expectations)

Adam: "When delegating a task, we should clarify its purpose, the required steps, the criteria for evaluating the results, and the deadlines. Can anyone share an example of a successfully delegated task?"

Youssef: "Yes, in a recent project, I delegated the task of testing the new system to one of the developers. I provided all the details and necessary support, and we followed up regularly. The result was excellent, and the task was completed on time and with high quality."

Adam: "That's a great example, Yusuf. Now, let's move on to providing support. What do we mean by support and how can we ensure employees have everything they need?"

Leila: "Support can be providing resources, ongoing training, or even continuous guidance. I think we need to identify the type of support each employee needs individually."

Adam: "Right. Support should be tailored to each task and each employee, as different employees may need different types of support. Let's look at how to give feedback."

(Displays a slide on giving feedback)

Adam: "Feedback should be constructive and focus on performance improvement. It should be timely and focus on modifiable behaviors. Can anyone share an experience where feedback was effective?"

Leila: "Once, I had an employee who was submitting reports late. I sat with him and discussed the reasons and possible solutions. I gave him constructive feedback on how to improve his time management. After that, his performance improved significantly."

Adam: "Great, Leila. That's an excellent example of how to give feedback effectively. In conclusion, let's remember that delegation is not just about distributing burdens, but it's also an opportunity to develop the team and build their capabilities. Can someone remind me of the basics of effective delegation? "

Choosing the right person for each task is the first step to effective delegation. Yusuf said:
"We need to know the strengths and weaknesses of each team member. Only then can we delegate tasks in a way that ensures success."

Clarifying expectations through good communication is essential in task delegation. Kareem said:
"There must be complete clarity about what is required, deadlines, and expected standards."

Providing support and resources for successful task delegation, leaders must provide the necessary support and resources for employees. Leila said:
"We need to ensure our employees have everything they need to execute tasks well."

(Adam ends the presentation)

Adam: "Thank you all for participating. Now, we have a practical exercise where you will delegate a real task within your teams and follow through on its execution using the tools we discussed today."

(Everyone begins the practical exercise)

Effective Delegation Techniques

During the workshop, several techniques for effective task delegation were reviewed:

1. **Choosing the Right People:**
   - Identify suitable tasks and delegate them to individuals with the necessary skills and experience.
   - Ensure the delegated employee has a clear understanding of the tasks and responsibilities required.
2. **Clearly Defining Goals:**
   - Clarify the goals and expected outcomes of the delegated tasks.
   - Provide clear instructions and set the criteria by which performance will be measured.
3. **Providing Support and Assistance:**
   - Ensure the employee has the resources and tools needed to execute the tasks.
   - Offer guidance and assistance when needed without micromanaging the details of the work.
4. **Monitoring and Evaluating:**
   - Regularly monitor the progress of the work and provide constructive feedback.
   - Assess the employee's performance and offer feedback to foster continuous improvement.

Website Development Project
Leila was delegated to be responsible for developing the company's new website.

She identified the right team, clarified expectations, and provided the necessary resources.

She regularly monitored progress and provided constructive feedback, leading to the successful and timely launch of the website.

Marketing Campaign Management
Youssef was tasked with managing a new marketing campaign. He effectively delegated tasks among team members, helping to execute the campaign efficiently and achieve excellent results.

In one task, Adam assigned a critical task to a new employee without ensuring their readiness. This led to project delays and the loss of some clients. This dramatic turning point made Adam realize the importance of ensuring employee readiness before delegating critical tasks, as well as consulting the department manager in selecting employees.

Delegation System
Clearly Defining Responsibilities
Adam established a system for clearly defining responsibilities. The project was divided into specific tasks, each assigned to an individual with set deadlines.

Monitoring Progress and Providing Feedback
Adam implemented a system for regularly monitoring progress and providing feedback. He said, "We need to make sure we track progress and provide constructive feedback in a timely manner."

Unfortunately, despite all the training, there was a delay in task completion. When the issue of the delay was raised, tension arose among the managers over who should take responsibility.

Leila felt the responsibility lay with the new employee, while Youssef believed it was the managers' fault for not providing enough support.
Sarah argued that the responsibility lay with the person who delegated the task without ensuring competence.

"We need to take responsibility for our decisions and learn from our mistakes. We must ensure our employees are ready before assigning them critical tasks," Adam said firmly.

The positive results from applying effective delegation systems and improving delegation skills
 included a significant improvement in team performance and productivity. For example:

- **New Product Development Project:** The project was completed with high efficiency thanks to effective delegation.
- **Improved Customer Satisfaction:** Customer satisfaction increased due to better and faster task execution.

Lessons Learned:

1. **Importance of Delegation in Improving Productivity:**
   - Proper delegation enables managers to focus on strategic goals.
   - Enhances team capabilities and increases employee satisfaction.
2. **Choosing the Right People:**
   - Identify appropriate tasks and delegate them to individuals with the necessary skills.
   - Ensure the employee understands the tasks and responsibilities required.
3. **Clearly Defining Goals:**
   - Provide clear instructions and set performance measurement criteria.
   - Ensure the employee knows the expected outcomes.
4. **Providing Support and Assistance:**
   - Provide the necessary resources and tools to execute tasks.
   - Offer guidance and assistance when needed without micromanaging.
5. **Monitoring and Evaluation:**
   - Regularly monitor progress and provide constructive feedback.
   - Assess performance and offer comments to promote continuous improvement.

Tools and Practical Exercises:
Tool: Task Delegation Plan Template

1. **Identify Tasks:** What tasks need to be delegated?
2. **Choose the Right Person:** Who is the best person to execute each task?
3. **Clarify Expectations:** What are the required expectations and standards?
4. **Provide Support:** What resources and support are needed to execute tasks?
5. **Monitor Progress:** How will progress be monitored and feedback provided?

Exercise: Delegation Skills Workshop

Gather your team in a workshop to improve delegation skills. Present short lectures on the basics of effective delegation, then divide the team into small groups to practice these skills through real-life scenarios.

Inspirational Quotes

"Effective delegation is the foundation of effective leadership." - Stephen Covey

"Trusting your team is the first step towards successful delegation." - Richard Branson

---

Discussion Questions

1. How can the task delegation process be improved in your team?
2. What challenges do you face when delegating tasks, and how can they be overcome?
3. How can sufficient support be ensured for employees when tasks are delegated?

Chapter Five: Training and Continuous Development

The Importance of Investing in Employee Development

When Adam took on the role of CEO, he realized that employee development was one of the key pillars for achieving long-term success. He saw that employees were the company's most important assets and that investing in their skill development would enhance their productivity and increase their commitment to the company. He believed that a work environment that encouraged continuous learning would create a team capable of adapting to rapid market changes and continuously innovating.

Building Effective Training Programs

To implement his vision, Adam decided to organize comprehensive training programs covering all aspects of work. He held a meeting with his team to discuss how to build these programs.

Adam: "Thank you all for coming. Today, we want to talk about how to build effective training programs that help us achieve our vision. Sarah, can you provide some ideas?"

Sarah: "Of course, Adam. I think we need to analyze the training needs of each department first. We can conduct surveys and interviews with employees to identify the areas where they need to improve their skills."

Kareem: "Also, we can invite experts from outside the company to conduct training workshops in specialized fields. This will help bring in new ideas and modern methods of working."

Leila: "Yes, and I think it's also important to offer internal training sessions led by experienced employees within the company. This will contribute to knowledge sharing and motivate employees."

Youssef: "Let's not forget about training on modern technologies. We should have ongoing training programs to learn about new software and tools emerging in the market."

Adam: "Excellent. Let's start by developing a detailed plan that includes a training needs analysis, identifying topics and trainers, and setting a training schedule. Sarah, can you take on this project?"

Sarah: "Absolutely, Adam. I'll start right away with preparing the surveys and interviews with employees."

During the implementation of the training programs, the company faced some challenges. There was a difference in opinions among the managers about how to allocate training resources.

Leila: "We need to focus on training vital departments first to ensure a quick return on investment."

Youssef: "But all departments need training equally to avoid any decline in performance."

Sarah: "I think we should start with the vital departments but not neglect the others. We can implement a phased training schedule that includes all departments in rotation."

Workshop: Building Effective Training Programs

Sarah and her team held a workshop to design a comprehensive training program covering all aspects of work. They started by identifying training needs through surveys and interviews with employees and managers. The workshop focused on the following elements:

1. **Training Needs Assessment:**
   - Conducted an analysis to identify current skill gaps and areas needing improvement.
   - Analyzed current performance and set future goals to guide the training program.
2. **Designing Training Programs:**
   - Developed training courses tailored to various employee levels, from beginners to executives.
   - Included a wide range of topics such as modern technology, management skills, and customer service.
3. **Implementing Training Programs:**
   - Delivered courses through a variety of methods, including in-person sessions, online courses, and interactive workshops.
   - Engaged experts and specialists to provide training and ensure content quality.
4. **Evaluating Training Effectiveness:**
   - Established mechanisms to assess the effectiveness of training programs

through post-training surveys and actual employee performance evaluations.
- Conducted periodic evaluations to improve programs and ensure the achievement of desired goals.

Long-Term Benefits of Continuous Development

The company began implementing the training and development programs, and the results were evident. Adam and his team noticed an increase in employee productivity and improvement in work quality. Employees became more capable of adapting to rapid market changes and more prepared to innovate and offer new solutions.

One notable example was the marketing department. After a series of trainings on digital analytics tools, the team increased the effectiveness of their advertising campaigns by 30%.

Leila was also able to reduce operating costs thanks to training on advanced financial analysis tools.

Adam held a meeting to review the impact of these programs on the company.

Adam: "Hello everyone. I wanted us to meet today to review the impact of the training programs we have implemented over the past few months. Sarah, can you provide a report on the results?"

Sarah: "Certainly, Adam. We have observed a 15% increase in employee productivity and a 10% reduction in error rates. Additionally, the survey showed that 85%

of employees are satisfied with the training programs and find them useful for developing their skills."

Kareem: "These are great results. I have also noticed an improvement in the marketing team's performance and their ability to effectively use new tools."

Leila: "I have also noticed an improvement in financial efficiency thanks to training on advanced financial tools."

Youssef: "In the technology department, we have become more capable of adopting and implementing new technologies quickly and efficiently."

Adam: "This is excellent. These results confirm that our investment in employee development was the right step. Let's continue to improve and develop our training programs to ensure we stay ahead. Remember, training is not just a cost; it is an investment in our future."

Everyone: "Agreed, Adam."

Lessons Learned:

1. **Importance of Investing in Employee Development:**
    - Continuous training and development enhance employee efficiency and job satisfaction.
    - Companies that invest in developing their employees enjoy higher retention rates and better productivity.
2. **Building Effective Training Programs:**
    - Assessing training needs helps design targeted and effective training programs.

- A variety of training methods (in-person, online, interactive) meet different needs and enhance training effectiveness.
3. **Evaluating Training Effectiveness:**
   - Regular evaluation of training programs ensures goals are met and programs are continuously improved.
   - Post-training surveys and actual performance assessments help measure training effectiveness and identify areas for improvement.
4. **Long-Term Benefits of Continuous Development:**
   - Continuous training leads to improved employee performance and increased productivity.
   - Employee development enhances job satisfaction, reducing employee turnover rates and improving the overall work environment.

To ensure a return on investment from employee training and development, measure performance improvement, reduce employee turnover by tracking turnover rates, and increase customer satisfaction.

Tools and Practical Exercises

To ensure the application of ideas gained from the training, here are some practical exercises such as:

- **Simulation Workshops:** To apply new skills in a realistic work environment.
- **Daily Challenges:** To motivate employees to use what they have learned in their daily tasks.
- **Regular Review Sessions:** To discuss progress and exchange ideas on how to improve performance.

Inspirational Quotes

"An investment in knowledge pays the best interest." - Benjamin Franklin

---

Discussion Questions

1. How can we ensure the long-term effectiveness of training programs?
2. What are some ways to encourage employees to adopt new skills?
3. How can we balance training different departments without disrupting daily operations?

Chapter Six: Motivation and Accountability

As Tech Excel continued to evolve and began implementing its strategic and tactical plans, Adam realized that motivation and accountability were crucial for sustaining success, achieving goals, and improving performance.

The challenge was to find the right balance between motivating employees to increase productivity while maintaining a high level of oversight to ensure goals were met.

Adam: "Hello everyone. Today, we want to discuss our team's overall performance and how we can improve it. Let's start by hearing your thoughts on the methods we use to manage teams and achieve goals. Kareem, what do you think?"

Kareem (Marketing Manager): "I believe that oversight is necessary to ensure adherence to standards and timelines. Therefore, I always follow every detail of the work closely because I think this maintains quality and prevents errors."

Leila (Finance Manager): "I agree with you, Kareem. In finance, we need great accuracy, so we also apply strict oversight. We use daily tracking schedules and detailed reports to ensure we stick to budgets and deadlines."

Youssef (Technology Manager): "From my perspective, motivation is key. We need a team that feels inspired and creative. I focus on giving teams freedom in their work and encouraging them to innovate. I believe that trust in the team yields better long-term results."

Hala (Public Relations Manager): "I lean towards motivation too, but I see oversight as necessary to ensure work quality. We use tools to track progress and identify areas for improvement, but I always try to make this part of the motivation process, not just oversight."

Sarah (HR Manager): "For me, the balance between motivation and oversight is essential. We need to implement motivational programs like performance rewards and public recognition, alongside closely monitoring performance to ensure goals are met. I believe that appreciation and motivation drive employees more than strict oversight."

Fatima (Financial Analysis Manager): "In financial analysis, we find that the balance between oversight and motivation can be achieved by setting clear and specific goals for each team. This way, everyone knows what is expected of them and feels accountable, but they also have the freedom to be motivated and innovate."

Nada (Digital Marketing Manager): "In digital marketing, we need to move quickly and adapt our strategies constantly. So, I give my team a lot of space for creativity and experimentation, but I ensure we track results regularly to make sure we're on the right path."

Omar (Marketing Analyst): "I think that collecting and analyzing data can help us achieve a balance between oversight and motivation. When we better understand our performance, we can provide constructive feedback and motivate the team to achieve new goals."

Maya (Training Manager): "From my perspective, we can use training as a tool to enhance both motivation and oversight. By continuously training employees, we ensure they have the necessary skills and feel supported, which enhances their performance and reduces the need for strict oversight."

Adam: "Thank you all for your input. It is clear that there is a diversity of approaches among us. Some prefer strict oversight, while others see motivation as the most important. We need to find a way to combine both approaches to ensure we achieve our goals without the team feeling pressured or losing motivation. I will work with you to develop a plan that balances oversight and motivation to ensure the best possible performance for the company. We will meet again. Thank you all."

The Challenge: Finding the Balance Between Motivation and Supervision

Adam: "Thank you for attending today. We want to discuss how to balance supervision and motivation to ensure the best performance from our team. It's clear that we have varying approaches. So, let's hear your suggestions on how to improve this situation. Kareem, what do you think?"

Kareem (Marketing Manager): "I think we need to set clear performance standards and precisely define goals so everyone knows what is expected of them. We can also use technological tools to track progress and reduce the need for direct supervision."

Leila (Finance Manager): "I agree with Kareem. Clear standards and technological tools can help. Additionally, we can organize regular follow-up meetings to discuss progress and solve problems as they arise, rather than waiting for them to accumulate."

Youssef (Technology Manager): "From my perspective, we can improve motivation by giving teams more autonomy. We can set the goals and let the teams choose the method that suits them best to achieve these goals. This will make them feel trusted and responsible."

Hala (Public Relations Manager): "I believe the balance can be achieved by enhancing communication between teams and management. We can hold regular feedback sessions to provide motivation and recognition on one hand, and identify areas that need improvement on the other."

Sarah (HR Manager): "I think we can use a reward system to encourage good performance. Employees need to see that their efforts are appreciated and rewarded. Additionally, we can implement training programs to develop the necessary skills to improve performance."

Fatima (Financial Analysis Manager): "I agree that motivation and supervision should go hand in hand. We can use performance reports to analyze progress and provide constructive feedback. This helps teams understand how they are progressing and encourages them to improve."

Nada (Digital Marketing Manager): "In digital marketing, we rely heavily on experimentation and analysis. Therefore, we can use data to motivate the team. When the team sees the impact of their efforts clearly, it will increase their motivation to achieve more."

Omar (Marketing Analyst): "We need to set up a system to regularly track goals and results. This will allow us to know if we are heading in the right direction and provide timely feedback and motivation."

Maya (Training Manager): "We can offer training programs focused on effective delegation and leadership development. This will give managers the tools they need to apply supervision and motivation in a balanced way."

Adam: "Excellent, these are great ideas. Based on what we've heard, I'll propose the following steps:
1. Set clear performance standards and goals for each team.
2. Use technological tools to track progress and performance reports.
3. Organize regular follow-up meetings to discuss progress and solve problems.
4. Implement a reward system to motivate good performance.
5. Enhance communication between teams and management.
6. Offer training programs to develop leadership skills and effective delegation.

This way, we can combine supervision and motivation to ensure goal achievement and maintain team enthusiasm. What do you think?"

Everyone: "Agreed!"

Adam: "Great! Let's start implementing these steps and monitor how things improve. But before that, let's study the matter seriously and ensure its quality. Thank you all for your valuable contributions."

Workshop: Building a Culture of Motivation and Accountability

Adam held a workshop with his team to discuss how to balance motivation and supervision.

The workshop began with examples of successful companies that achieved this balance and how it improved their performance and employee satisfaction.

Adam: "Hello everyone, thank you for coming today. Today, we will discuss how to build a company culture that combines motivation and accountability. Let's start with examples of successful companies that have effectively achieved this balance."

Kareem: "Through my research, I found that Google has significantly achieved this balance. By providing a work environment that encourages innovation and gives employees the freedom to make decisions, they saw tangible results in increased productivity and creativity."

Leila: "Apple has also managed to combine motivation and accountability by setting clear goals and using a performance-based reward system. This approach helped motivate employees to achieve goals accurately and efficiently."

Youssef: "At Facebook, they used data analytics to track performance and continuously improve processes. This strategy was beneficial in motivating teams and holding them accountable for their set goals."

Hala: "Examples like these show that balancing motivation and accountability not only concerns achieving managerial goals but also affects employee satisfaction and builds a positive work culture."

Sarah: "From an HR perspective, companies like Zappos have provided unique benefits to enhance motivation, such as unlimited vacations and work flexibility. These policies helped build a motivated and accountable environment."

Fatima: "In my analysis of tech companies, I found that using financial analytics to track performance and provide regular reports can greatly benefit performance management and team motivation."

Nada: "As a digital marketing manager, I see that continuous innovation and experimentation play a big role in building a culture of motivation and accountability. We should strive to encourage creativity while closely monitoring results."

Omar: "From my marketing experience, we can use continuous monitoring and evaluation systems to help teams focus on strategic goals and achieve them effectively."

Maya: "As a training manager, I encourage offering advanced training programs aimed at enhancing leadership skills and boosting creativity within teams. These programs naturally promote motivation and accountability."

Adam: "Thank you all for your valuable participation. Based on what we heard, we now want to apply these ideas in our company. We will set clear performance standards, use tech tools to track progress, organize regular follow-up meetings, develop training programs, and establish a reward system that enhances performance and creativity. Do you have any other suggestions before we start?"

Everyone: "We agree and are ready to cooperate!"

Adam: "Great! Let's start working on implementing these steps and maintain the spirit of cooperation and motivation in all company departments. Thank you again for your efforts."

Setting Motivation Goals
Motivation Workshops
Leila began by holding a workshop with the team to identify core motivation goals. The team came up with a list of motivation goals that include:
- Improving performance and productivity.
- Enhancing loyalty and belonging to the company.
- Encouraging innovation and creativity.
- Supporting professional and personal development for employees.

"We need to ensure that every employee feels valued and has the opportunity to grow and develop," Leila emphasized the importance of supporting professional development.

Developing the Motivation System
Establishing a Reward System Kareem suggested
establishing a reward system that enhances good performance and motivates employees to achieve goals. The system included:
- Financial rewards for outstanding performance.
- Recognition programs for employees who show dedication and creativity.
- Opportunities for professional development such as training courses and workshops.

"Rewards are not just about money; it's about feeling appreciated and belonging," Kareem pointed out the importance of non-financial aspects of motivation.

Implementing Accountability Systems
Setting Performance Standards
Youssef presented a plan to implement accountability systems based on clear and measurable performance standards. The plan included:
- Defining Key Performance Indicators (KPIs) for each role.
- Regular performance evaluations.
- Semi-annual review sessions to discuss progress and challenges.

"Accountability means we are all responsible for achieving the set goals and working transparently," Youssef explained the importance of clarity in performance standards.

Executing Motivation and Accountability Systems
Follow-Up and Motivation Meetings
The teams began implementing the motivation and accountability systems. Leila organized monthly follow-

up meetings to review progress and motivate the teams to maintain good performance.

"We need to stay in constant communication and continue to provide support and appreciation for everyone," Leila said in one of the follow-up meetings.

Effective Motivation System
Examples of Positive Results from Implementing These Systems

For instance, the marketing team succeeded in significantly increasing the number of new clients after implementing the new motivation system. Financial rewards and recognition programs were a major driving force for them to achieve this success.

Ali's Success Story:

Ali, one of the project managers in the company, faced challenges in managing his team and achieving goals. Through regular evaluations and constructive feedback, he improved his leadership skills and developed his team. Ali became an effective leader, and his team achieved remarkable successes in several projects, leading to improved customer satisfaction and increased revenue.

Overall Performance Improvement:

After implementing the rewards and recognition system, Adam noticed a significant improvement in employee performance and an increase in enthusiasm and motivation. The company became more capable of achieving its strategic goals and increasing its market share. Enhancing team spirit through group activities improved the work environment and increased employee satisfaction.

Motivation and Accountability System
How to Balance Motivation and Control
1. **Set Clear and Defined Goals:**
   - Clear goals help guide the team's efforts and enhance the sense of achievement when they are met.
   - Performance standards were established for each employee and linked to the company's overall goals.
2. **Encourage Individual Initiatives:**
   - Supporting new ideas and individual initiatives fosters innovation and motivation.
   - Rewards and recognition are given to employees who show outstanding performance or present innovative ideas.
3. **Provide Constructive Feedback:**
   - Continuous feedback helps employees understand their strengths and weaknesses and work on improving them.
   - Feedback should be constructive and aimed at improving performance, not negative criticism.
4. **Provide a Stimulating Work Environment:**
   - Creating a work environment that encourages cooperation and positive interaction among employees.
   - Organizing events and activities that enhance team spirit and strengthen relationships among employees.

Systems to Motivate the Team and Achieve Accountability

1. **Rewards and Recognition System:**
   - A rewards system based on performance and achievements was developed, including financial and non-financial rewards such as certificates of appreciation and training opportunities.
   - Outstanding employees are recognized at monthly company meetings to foster a positive competitive spirit.
2. **Regular Evaluation System:**
   - A regular evaluation system was implemented to review employee performance regularly and identify areas for improvement.
   - Semi-annual review sessions are organized to discuss progress and achieve set goals.
3. **Group Accountability System:**
   - Group accountability mechanisms are applied where goals are achieved as a team, not just as individuals.
   - Enhancing team spirit and cooperation through shared responsibility for project success.

Lessons Learned:
1. **Balancing Motivation and Supervision:**
   - Motivation boosts productivity and creativity, while supervision ensures goals are met and performance levels are maintained.
   - Supervision should be based on trust and support, not control and pressure.
2. **Effective Motivation and Accountability Systems:**
   - Reward and recognition systems foster positive competition and increase employee satisfaction.
   - Regular evaluations help identify areas for improvement and enhance continuous performance.
   - Group accountability strengthens team spirit and collaboration.
3. **Examples of Positive Outcomes:**
   - Individual and group success stories highlight the importance of motivation and accountability in achieving goals.
   - Improving the work environment and increasing employee satisfaction lead to overall company performance improvement.

Tools and Practical Exercises
Tool: Motivation and Accountability Plan Template
1. **Defining Motivation Goals:** What are the main goals we seek to achieve through motivation?
2. **Setting Performance Standards:** What standards will we use to evaluate performance?
3. **Designing a Rewards System:** How will we reward outstanding performance?
4. **Implementing Monitoring Systems:** How will we ensure progress tracking and goal achievement?

Exercise: Motivation and Accountability Workshop
Gather your team for a workshop to develop a motivation and accountability system. Start by defining goals and standards, then design a rewards system that suits your team's needs. Conclude with a discussion session on how to effectively implement these systems.

Inspirational Quotes
"Motivation is what gets you started. Habit is what keeps you going." - Jim Rohn

"Accountability is the acknowledgment that everyone must be responsible for their actions." - Patrick Lencioni

---

Discussion Questions
1. How can you improve the motivation system in your team?
2. What challenges do you face when implementing accountability systems, and how can they be overcome?
3. How can you ensure a balance between motivation and accountability to achieve goals?

Chapter Seven: Continuous Improvement and Innovation

As the company progressed in achieving its goals, Adam and his team realized that continuous improvement and innovation were key to maintaining growth and market superiority. It was necessary to create an environment that encouraged creative thinking and regularly implemented improvements.

Instilling a Culture of Continuous Improvement
Identifying Areas for Improvement

Adam held a new meeting with the leadership team to discuss how to instill a culture of continuous improvement within the company. The meeting was attended by key managers as well as some employees from different departments.

"We need to make continuous improvement a part of our daily culture. This requires everyone's commitment to constantly seek ways to improve performance and innovate in their work," Adam said as he opened the meeting.

Youssef: "Yes, absolutely. Let's start by identifying areas that need improvement. Can we look at our current performance and pinpoint the areas we can enhance?"

Adam: "Agreed, let's begin by reviewing our performance and identifying the points we need to focus on."

The meeting then started with a session to identify areas that needed improvement. Youssef led the session, where the team reviewed the current performance and identified points for improvement.

"We need to be honest with ourselves and identify the weaknesses we can improve," Youssef said, emphasizing the importance of transparency at this stage. "I believe it is important to start by discussing internal processes. I have analyzed our current efficiency and productivity levels, and there are some opportunities to improve processes, especially regarding streamlining procedures and better resource allocation."

Fatima: "I agree with you, Youssef. Additionally, there is an urgent need to enhance training on new processes and update them regularly to ensure we are up-to-date with the latest industry practices."

Leila: "Regarding customer service, we desperately need to improve our response time and service quality. Are there any suggestions on how we can achieve this better?"

Maya: "We can develop a system to track response time and processing of customer requests, as well as enhance communication with customers throughout all service stages to ensure their satisfaction."

Omar: "Regarding technology, can we think about updating current systems and using new technological tools? This could help improve our efficiency and provide more data for decision-making."

Sarah: "I agree with you, Omar. We should invest in training our team on the new systems and how to use them effectively."

Adam: "Great, thank you all for the valuable input. We will now set specific action steps for each of these areas and hold regular follow-up meetings to review progress. Are there any other questions or comments before we conclude?"

Examples of Areas for Improvement
- Internal Processes: Improving efficiency and productivity.
- Customer Service: Enhancing response speed and service quality.
- Technology: Updating systems and using new tools.
- Marketing: Developing new strategies to reach customers.

Encouraging Innovation
Innovation Workshops
Leila organized workshops to foster innovation among employees. These workshops included brainstorming sessions and pilot projects to implement new ideas.

"Innovation comes from everyone. We must encourage every employee to contribute their ideas and participate in improving the company," said Leila, emphasizing the importance of collective participation in innovation.

Implementing Improvements and Innovations

Executing Improvements

After identifying areas for improvement and encouraging innovation, the teams began implementing improvements and innovations in their daily operations. Kareem led the marketing team in executing new marketing strategies, while Youssef led the technology team in updating systems and improving processes.

"Execution is key. We need to ensure we implement improvements effectively and continuously evaluate their impact," said Adam.

Monitoring Improvements

Improvement Follow-Up Meetings

Sarah organized regular follow-up meetings to review progress and assess the impact of the improvements and innovations. These meetings included discussions on successes, challenges, and ways to continuously improve performance.

"We need to be flexible and ready to adjust our plans based on the results we get," said Sarah.

Successful Innovation

The technology team developed a new app that enhanced customer experience and loyalty. Meanwhile, the customer service team improved response times to complaints, leading to increased customer satisfaction.

From these lessons learned, a deeper understanding of the importance of this process and how to successfully implement it in the workplace can be derived.

1. **Importance of Organizational Culture:**
   - **Continuous Improvement Culture:** Promoting a culture that encourages continuous improvement at all levels of the company.
   - **Transparency and Openness:** The importance of transparency and openness to new ideas from all employees.
2. **Regular Evaluation and Analysis:**
   - **Performance Analysis:** Conducting regular performance evaluations to identify strengths and weaknesses.
   - **Using Data:** How to use data and analytics to make informed decisions.
3. **Technology and Innovation:**
   - **Adopting Technology:** Benefits of adopting new technologies to enhance efficiency and productivity.
   - **Investing in R&D:** The importance of investing in research and development to stay competitive.
4. **Training and Development:**
   - **Continuous Training:** The importance of providing continuous training programs to keep up with technological and industrial changes.
   - **Skills Development:** How to develop employees' skills to meet new challenges.
5. **Change Management:**
   - **Adapting to Change:** The importance of adapting to changes in the market and technology.
   - **Engaging Employees:** Involving employees in the change process to ensure its success.

6. **Team Collaboration:**
   - **Effective Communication:** The importance of effective communication between different teams to improve processes.
   - **Teamwork:** Promoting teamwork to solve problems and innovate.
7. **Inspirational Leadership:**
   - **Leadership Role:** How inspirational leadership affects employee motivation and encourages innovation.
   - **Guidance and Support:** The importance of providing continuous guidance and support to teams.
8. **Motivation and Rewards:**
   - **Reward System:** Developing a reward system that encourages innovation and continuous improvement.
   - **Recognizing Efforts:** Acknowledging employees' innovative efforts and encouraging them to continue their good work.
9. **Strategic Planning:**
   - **Setting Goals:** How to set clear strategic goals for improvement and innovation.
   - **Creating Tactical Plans:** Developing tactical plans to achieve strategic goals.
10. **Learning from Mistakes:**
    - **Learning from Failure:** The importance of learning from mistakes and failures as part of the continuous improvement process.
    - **Failure Analysis:** How to analyze failures and draw lessons from them to improve future processes.

Tools and Practical Exercises
Tool: Continuous Improvement Plan Template
1. Identify areas for improvement: What areas need improvement?
2. Set goals: What goals do we want to achieve through improvement?
3. Develop an improvement plan: What steps will we take to improve performance?
4. Implement improvements: How will we apply the improvements in daily work?
5. Follow up on improvements: How will we evaluate the impact of the improvements and make necessary adjustments?

Exercise: Innovation Workshop
Gather your team in a workshop to identify new ideas and possible improvements. Use brainstorming sessions and pilot projects to implement new ideas and evaluate their impact.

Inspirational Quotes
"Continuous improvement is the foundation of lasting success." - W. Edwards Deming

"Innovation distinguishes between a leader and a follower." - Steve Jobs

---

Discussion Questions
1. How can the processes in your team be improved to achieve greater efficiency?
2. What new ideas can be applied to enhance innovation in your work?
3. How can we ensure that improvements are effectively implemented and their impact continuously monitored?

Chapter Eight: Adapting and Responding to Changes

As "Tech Excel" continued to grow and expand into new markets and as markets evolved, Adam realized that the ability to adapt to rapid changes in the business environment was essential for maintaining success and excellence. However, adapting to change requires flexible thinking and effective strategies to handle sudden shifts. The biggest challenge he faced was how to make the company and its employees resilient and able to adapt to the new challenges and opportunities that constantly arise.

Facing Challenges
The Importance of Flexibility in the Workplace and Adapting to Change

Adam held an extensive meeting with the leadership team to discuss strategies for adapting to change. The meeting was attended by all key managers, as well as some employees from different departments.

Adam spoke about the importance of flexibility in the workplace. He emphasized that companies capable of quickly adapting to changes have a significant competitive advantage. He pointed to examples from major tech companies that have succeeded in staying at the forefront of the market due to their ability to adapt to innovations and changes.

Adam: "Thank you all for being here today. As you know, we live in a rapidly changing world, and the companies that can adapt to these changes are the ones that achieve sustainable success. Today, we want to talk about the importance of flexibility in the workplace and how we can be more prepared to adapt to any changes that occur in the market or within our company."

Leila: "I completely agree with you, Adam. We have seen many major companies like Amazon and Google stay ahead because of their ability to quickly adapt to innovations and changes. But how do we start applying this concept here in our company?"

Adam: "Let's start by understanding that we need to change our mindset towards change. Instead of seeing it as a threat, we should view it as an opportunity for growth. Youssef, how do you see the role of technology in enhancing our flexibility?"

Youssef: "Technology plays a vital role. We need to be ready to adopt new systems and tools that help us improve our efficiency. For example, we can use AI technologies to analyze data faster and make smarter decisions."

Sarah: "For human resources, I believe we need continuous training programs to equip employees with new skills. This will help them adapt to technical and operational changes."

Kareem: "From a marketing perspective, we need to be ready to quickly adjust our strategies based on new market trends. We should be more flexible in our marketing plans and respond swiftly to changes in customer preferences."

Hala: "From a public relations standpoint, constant communication with clients and partners is crucial. We need to be transparent about the changes we are making and how they will affect them. This will build trust and strengthen our relationship with them."

Adam: "These are excellent points. Now, let's identify some practical steps we can take to enhance our flexibility.
First, we need to establish cross-functional teams that can handle different challenges quickly and effectively.
Second, we should develop a culture of continuous learning and encourage employees to acquire new skills."

Fatima: "From a financial perspective, we need to be prepared to reallocate resources quickly when necessary. We must be flexible with our budgets and work on reducing bureaucracy that could hinder quick decision-making."

Maya: "For training, we can organize regular workshops focusing on developing flexibility and adaptability skills. We can also invite external experts to provide new insights on how to adapt to changes."

Adam: "Exactly. Finally, we need to establish a continuous feedback system from all departments. This will help us identify any issues or opportunities for development early on. Let's commit to these initiatives and be a model for companies that successfully adapt to change."

Youssef: "Thank you, Adam. I believe we are all committed to achieving this goal. Let's start working on these initiatives immediately."

Adam: "Thank you all. I am confident that our collaboration will lead to the flexibility we need for sustainable success."

Analyzing Market Changes
Market Analysis Session
The meeting started with a session analyzing market changes. Kareem led this session, where the team reviewed current data and future forecasts to identify trends and potential changes.

"We need to be aware of what is happening around us. Market changes can be opportunities or threats, and we need to be prepared for both," said Kareem, emphasizing the importance of readiness.

Developing Adaptation Strategies
Formulating Adaptation Strategies
After analyzing market changes, the team developed strategies to adapt to these changes. The strategies included plans to deal with new competition, changes in customer preferences, and technological advancements.

Examples of Adaptation Strategies
- Continuous innovation: Developing new products and services to meet changing market needs.
- Enhancing customer relationships: Increasing communication with customers to understand their needs and provide tailored solutions.

- Improving efficiency: **Reevaluating internal processes to improve efficiency and reduce costs.**
- Diversifying markets: **Entering new markets to reduce dependence on a single market.**

Implementing Adaptation Strategies
Applying Strategies
After identifying adaptation strategies, the teams began implementing these strategies in their daily operations.
Leila led the finance team in developing new financial models to support expansion into new markets,
while Youssef led the technology team in adopting new technologies to keep up with technological changes.

"We need to be flexible and ready to adjust our plans based on the changes we face," said Adam, emphasizing the importance of flexibility in execution.

Monitoring Adaptation
Sarah organized regular follow-up meetings to review the progress of the strategies and assess their impact. These meetings included discussions on successes, challenges, and ways to continuously improve performance.

"Adapting to change is not a one-time process; it is a continuous process that requires constant monitoring and ongoing adjustments," said Sarah.

Successful Adaptation to Change
During the economic downturn, Tech Excel was affected like other companies. However, thanks to the adaptation strategies set by Adam, the company was able to quickly adjust its plans to reduce costs and increase efficiency.

Resources were reallocated, and some teams were restructured to ensure continued productivity. This quick response helped the company weather the crisis and remain strong in the market.

The marketing team successfully adjusted their strategies to face new competition, leading to a 15% increase in the company's market share. At the same time, the technology team successfully adopted new technologies that increased internal operational efficiency by 20%.

Strategies for Adapting to Rapid Changes

1. **Fostering a Culture of Change and Innovation:**
    - Adam encouraged the development of an organizational culture that supports innovation and embraces change.
    - Workshops and seminars were organized to promote innovative thinking and encourage employees to present new ideas.
2. **Continuous Learning and Professional Development:**
    - Continuous training programs were enhanced to equip employees with the skills needed to adapt to changes.
    - Employees were encouraged to attend external training courses and workshops to stay updated with the latest trends and technologies in their field.
3. **Continuous Market and Competitor Analysis:**
    - Specialized teams were formed to monitor market changes and analyze competitors' strategies.

- Regular reports were provided to senior management on new trends, potential challenges, and opportunities.
4. **Developing Flexible Strategies:**
    - Flexible strategic plans were created that could be quickly adjusted based on changing conditions.
    - Proactive thinking and the development of contingency plans were encouraged to address potential crises.
5. **Developing Adaptive Leadership Skills:**
    - Leaders were trained on how to manage change and adapt to changing circumstances.
    - Leadership skills in making quick decisions and handling pressure were strengthened.

Lessons Learned:

1. **The Importance of Flexibility in the Workplace:**
   - The ability to adapt to rapid changes gives companies a significant competitive advantage.
   - Embracing a culture of change and innovation helps enhance organizational flexibility.

2. **Strategies for Adapting to Rapid Changes:**
   - Promoting a culture of innovation and continuous learning helps improve adaptability.
   - Continuous market and competitor analysis helps identify opportunities and challenges early.
   - Developing flexible and proactive strategies enhances the ability to deal with crises.

3. **Success Stories of Effectively Dealing with Change:**
   - Success stories reflect the importance of adaptability and flexibility in achieving goals and projects.
   - Quick responses to challenges contribute to maintaining business continuity and achieving growth.

Tools and Practical Exercises
Tool: Change Adaptation Plan Template

1. **Identifying Changes:** What changes are we facing?
2. **Analyzing Impact:** What is the impact of these changes on the company?
3. **Developing Adaptation Strategies:** What strategies will we use to adapt to these changes?
4. **Implementing Strategies:** How will we apply these strategies in daily operations?
5. **Monitoring Adaptation:** How will we evaluate the impact of the strategies and make necessary adjustments?

Exercise: Change Adaptation Workshop

Gather your team in a workshop to identify potential changes and develop strategies to adapt to them. Use brainstorming sessions to analyze the impact and develop detailed plans for each team.

Inspirational Quotes

"Change is the law of life, and those who look only to the past or present are certain to miss the future." - John F. Kennedy

"It is not the strongest or the most intelligent who will survive but those who can best manage change." - Charles Darwin

---

Discussion Questions

1. How can your team adapt to rapid changes in the market?
2. What strategies can be used to adapt to unexpected challenges?
3. How can team resilience be enhanced to cope with change?

Chapter Nine: Leading by Example

As the company continued to grow and achieve success, Adam realized that the most crucial role of leadership was the ability to lead by example. As the CEO, his actions and attitudes significantly influenced the behavior and culture of the entire company. He wanted to be a role model, inspiring his team and instilling the values he upheld.

Leading by Example

Adam began the meeting with the leadership team by reminding them of the importance of leading by example. The meeting was attended by all the key managers as well as some principal employees. "Leadership is not just about giving orders, but being the model everyone follows. We must reflect the values we want to see in our company," Adam said as he opened the meeting.

Applying Values in Daily Work

Sarah talked about how to embody values in daily work through their behavior and actions. "We must be the first to adhere to the values we promote. Integrity, transparency, and collaboration must be part of our daily lives at work," Sarah said.

Being a Role Model

In the leadership team meeting, Adam encouraged the managers to share their personal stories about handling challenges with integrity. Kareem, the marketing director, started by sharing a story about a difficult situation he faced with his team and how he dealt with it with integrity, which had a positive impact on the team.

Kareem: "I would like to share a story from last year when we were launching a new marketing campaign. The pressure was immense, and the deadline was approaching fast. While reviewing the final materials, I discovered a major error in one of the main advertisements. We could have ignored the error and launched the campaign as it was, but I felt it was necessary to correct it."

Sarah: "What did you do at that time?"

Kareem: "I made a tough decision. I gathered my team and told them the truth. I said we had made a mistake and needed to fix it before launching the campaign. I knew this would mean working extra hours and possibly missing the deadline, but I was confident that integrity was paramount."

Leila: "How did the team react?"

Kareem: "At first, they were frustrated and angry. It wasn't easy for them to accept that the hard work they had done needed to be reconsidered. But after I explained the importance of integrity and how launching a campaign with an error could negatively affect our reputation, they began to understand."

Youssef: "And how did that impact the team in the end?"

Kareem: "When the team realized that I was willing to take responsibility and sacrifice the deadline for the sake of integrity, the atmosphere changed completely. We worked together for extra hours, ensured the error was corrected, and launched a flawless campaign. More importantly, the team felt proud of what we had accomplished, and their respect for me and for themselves grew."

Hala: "That's a great example of leading with integrity. How did that affect the team's performance afterward?"

Kareem: "The results were amazing. Not only did we meet our campaign goals, but we exceeded them. Morale improved, and the team became more cohesive and confident in their abilities. We all learned that integrity is not just a theoretical value but the foundation of our success at work."

Adam: "Thank you, Kareem, for sharing your story. It reminds us all of the importance of integrity and leading by example. We must always remember that our teams look to us for guidance, and we must be role models in how we handle challenges."

With this story, Kareem provided a real-life example of how to handle difficult situations with integrity, showing how such actions can boost team confidence and lead to better long-term results.

Building Trust

Achieving Trust through Actions
Leila emphasized the importance of building trust through actions, not just words.
 "Trust is built through consistent and reliable actions. We must always be honest and dependable in our dealings," said Leila.

Impact on Culture

Positive Impact on Company Culture

Youssef discussed the impact of leading by example on company culture.

"When employees see their leaders acting with integrity and transparency, they adopt the same behaviors. This creates a positive and cohesive culture within the company," said Youssef.

> A notable example was when Adam decided to reduce his salary during a difficult period for the company to support the budget and avoid laying off employees. This decision greatly enhanced employee trust and loyalty to the company.

Tools and Practical Exercises
Tool: Leading by Example Model

1. Identify Values: What core values do you want to reflect in your leadership?
2. Embody Values: How can you embody these values in your daily actions?
3. Promote Positive Behaviors: How can you encourage positive behaviors in your team?
4. Build Trust: What steps can be taken to build trust within the team?
5. Monitor Impact: How can you measure the impact of your leadership on the company culture?

Exercise: Leading by Example Workshop

Gather your team in a workshop to discuss and identify the core values that leadership should reflect. Use real-life stories and experiences to illustrate how these values can be embodied in daily work.

Inspirational Quotes

"Leadership is not just a title, but a responsibility to be a role model for others." - James M. Barrie

"Trust is the flower, leadership is the water, both need each other to flourish." - John C. Maxwell

---

Discussion Questions

1. How can leaders be good role models for their team?
2. What core values should leadership reflect in our company?
3. How can leading by example impact company culture and team performance?

Chapter Ten: Participation and Collective Decision-Making

Enhancing Participation at Tech Excel
After Tech Excel successfully adapted to rapid changes, Adam realized that enhancing employee participation in collective decision-making was the next step towards achieving sustainable success. He knew that involving employees in decision-making not only increased their satisfaction but also improved the quality of the decisions made.

The Challenge: Involving Everyone in the Decision-Making Process
In a leadership team meeting, Adam noticed that some managers were making decisions individually without consulting their teams. This approach led to some inappropriate decisions and negatively affected employee morale. It was clear that there was a need to enhance the collective decision-making process.

The Importance of Participation in Decision-Making
Adam began by explaining the importance of participation in decision-making. He pointed out that collective decisions are often more comprehensive and wise due to the diversity of ideas and experiences shared by team members. Additionally, participation enhances employees' commitment to implementing decisions as they feel part of the process.

Adam: "Thank you all for being here. Recently, I've noticed that some decisions are being made individually without consulting the team. This approach has negatively impacted employee morale and led to some inappropriate decisions. We need to enhance the collective decision-making process."

Sarah: "I agree with you, Adam. I believe that team participation in decision-making can improve the quality of decisions."

Kareem: "But sometimes, there's no time to consult everyone. How can we balance the need for quick decisions with team participation?"

Adam: "That's a good point, Kareem. We can find a balance by identifying the types of decisions that require collective input and those that can be made quickly. Strategic decisions, for example, should include the entire team, while simple daily decisions can be made individually."

Leila: "I agree. Team participation can bring different perspectives that may not be clear to an individual. Can we establish a clear process for collective decision-making?"

Youssef: "Yes, we can develop a structure that includes regular brainstorming sessions and short meetings to evaluate different options."

Hala: "I think using technological tools can facilitate this process. We can use online platforms for voting and idea sharing."

Adam: "Good idea, Hala. This will enable everyone to participate even if they aren't in the same place. Also, we need to promote a culture of transparency so that we all understand the reasons behind the decisions made."

Fatima: "Yes, transparency is important. We can provide regular reports explaining how decisions are made and the reasons behind them."

Nada: "And I think encouraging employees to express their opinions and ideas without fear of criticism will be a big step towards enhancing participation."

Omar: "We also need to organize training sessions to enhance collective decision-making skills among the team."

Maya: "I agree. We can organize workshops to train everyone in these skills and promote effective communication."

Adam: "Good. We'll start by identifying the types of decisions that require collective participation, developing a clear decision-making structure, and using appropriate technological tools. Let's all work together to promote this culture. Thank you all."

Workshop: Enhancing Collective Decision-Making

Adam held an interactive workshop to enhance collective decision-making practices. The workshop was divided into several sessions focusing on practical concepts and tools to promote participation.

Adam: "Welcome everyone, today we will conduct a workshop to enhance collective decision-making practices. We'll start by dividing the workshop into several sessions focusing on practical concepts and tools to promote participation. Let's begin with the first round."

Sarah: "What is the main goal of this first session, Adam?"

Adam: "The first session will address the concept of collective decision-making and the importance of involving all team members. I'll start by explaining how collective decisions are often more comprehensive and wise due to the diversity of ideas and experiences."

Kareem: "Can you give us an example of that, Adam?"

Adam: "Of course, Kareem. For instance, when we were planning to launch a new product, the decision-making process involved all departments. This led to an improved product thanks to the diverse ideas contributed by the entire team. Now let's talk about the tools we can use to enhance this participation."

Leila: "Can we talk about brainstorming sessions? How can we organize them effectively?"

Adam: "Certainly, Leila. Brainstorming sessions are a great tool. It's important to set a clear goal for the session and encourage all members to share their ideas freely without fear of criticism. We can also use the 'round-robin' technique where each member presents one idea in each round."

Youssef: "What about using technology? Are there tools that can help us enhance participation even when we are in different geographical locations?"

Adam: "Yes, Youssef. There are many technological tools such as online suggestion platforms and online voting tools. These tools make it easy to share ideas and vote on them quickly and efficiently."

Hala: "I wonder how we can ensure transparency in the decision-making process?"

Adam: "Transparency is key, Hala. We need to share information and data related to decisions with all team members. We can also explain the reasons behind each decision and the potential outcomes."

Fatima: "Can we develop a clear decision-making mechanism that includes all team members?"

Adam: "Absolutely, Fatima. We can define the roles and responsibilities of each member in the decision-making process and clarify the steps we will follow. This will help make the process more organized and efficient."

Nada: "What about regular meetings? Should we hold them regularly to follow up on progress?"

Adam: "Yes, Nada. Regular meetings are very important to review progress and evaluate impacts. We can hold monthly meetings to follow up on plans and adjust them as needed."

Omar: "How can we ensure that all ideas are heard and considered?"

Adam: "We need to encourage everyone to freely express their opinions and ideas. We can use techniques like the 'round-table' where each member is given the opportunity to speak without interruption."

Maya: "Can we provide training sessions to enhance collective decision-making skills among the team?"

Adam: "Yes, Maya. We will organize workshops and training sessions to enhance these skills and promote effective communication among the team."

Adam: "Alright, let's now move on to the practical session where we will apply some of these tools in real scenarios. Let's begin."

Strategies to Enhance Participation and Collective Decision-Making

1. **Create an Encouraging Environment for Participation:**
     - Encourage employees to express their opinions and ideas without fear of criticism.
     - Organize regular brainstorming sessions to generate ideas and solutions.
2. **Define a Clear Decision-Making Structure:**
     - Establish a clear decision-making mechanism that includes all team members.
     - Define the roles and responsibilities of each member in the decision-making process.
3. **Use Technological Tools to Enhance Participation:**
     - Use technological tools such as online suggestion and voting platforms.

- Organize virtual meetings to allow everyone to participate regardless of geographical location.
4. **Promote a Culture of Transparency:**
    - Share information and data related to decisions with all employees.
    - Explain the reasons behind decisions and their potential outcomes.

Adam: "Okay, let's start by defining a specific scenario we can work on. What is the first scenario we want to discuss?"

Sarah: "I think improving customer service is an important area. We can work on a scenario on how to handle a sudden increase in customer requests."

Adam: "Excellent. Let's start with this scenario. First, we'll use a brainstorming session to generate ideas. Remember, the goal is to come up with as many ideas as possible. Let's start with each of us proposing one idea."

Kareem: "We can create a dedicated team to handle excess requests during peak times."

Leila: "How about improving the automated response system to sort requests based on priority and importance?"

Youssef: "We can apply AI technology to analyze requests and suggest the most effective solutions."

Hala: "Increase employee training on crisis management and handling high pressure."

Fatima: "Use project management tools to track the progress of each request and ensure none are lost."

Nada: "Launch a dedicated app through which customers can track their requests and easily submit complaints or suggestions."

Omar: "Analyze previous data to identify the busiest periods and prepare with additional resources."

Maya: "Provide incentives for employees who manage to handle the most requests efficiently."

Adam: "Great! We now have a diverse set of ideas. Let's move on to the next step, which is voting on the most feasible ideas and prioritizing them.
 I'll use the online voting tool we discussed.
Each of you can vote on the ideas you believe will be the most effective."

(After Voting)

Adam: "Okay, the ideas that received the highest number of votes are:
- Creating a dedicated team to handle excess requests,
- Implementing AI technology to analyze requests,
- Launching a dedicated app for customers. Now, let's define the steps to implement these ideas."

Kareem: "I can take responsibility for forming the dedicated team, determining work schedules, and contact points."

Youssef: "I will take on the task of researching and implementing AI technology. I will need some time to identify the most suitable system and train the team to use it."

Nada: "I will work on developing the dedicated app in collaboration with the technology and marketing teams to ensure it meets customer needs."

Adam: "Excellent. Now we have a clear plan. Let's make sure to follow up on the progress of each idea periodically. Sarah, can you organize regular meetings to review the progress?"

Sarah: "Of course, I will schedule monthly meetings to evaluate the progress and provide the necessary reports."

Adam: "Great. So, we have a work plan and a follow-up system. Thank you all for your active contributions. This is a great example of how using collective decision-making can achieve tangible results. Let's continue working in the same spirit and apply these strategies in other areas."

Improving Internal Operations

In an attempt to improve internal operations, the management of "Tech Excel" decided to involve all employees in the improvement process. An online platform was created to collect suggestions and ideas from employees across all departments. Thanks to this initiative, several improvements were implemented, leading to increased efficiency and reduced costs.

Lessons Learned
1. **The Importance of Participation in Decision-Making:**
   - Participation enhances the quality of decisions and increases employee commitment to implementing them.
   - Collective decisions benefit from the diversity of ideas and experiences.
2. **Strategies to Enhance Participation:**
   - Creating an encouraging environment for participation helps gather diverse ideas and innovative solutions.
   - Using technological tools can enhance the effectiveness and ease of participation.
   - Transparency in the decision-making process builds trust and increases commitment.
3. **Success Stories Confirming the Effectiveness of Participation:**
   - Involving employees in decision-making leads to tangible improvements in products and processes.
   - Successful experiences reinforce the importance of adopting these practices sustainably.

By promoting employee participation in the collective decision-making process, Adam and his team at "Tech Excel" improved the quality of decisions and increased employee commitment to implementing them. This step was crucial in enhancing the company culture and achieving sustainable success, confirming that effective participation is the key to success in the modern workplace.

Tools and Practical Exercises

Tool: Decision-Making Participation Enhancement Plan Template

1. **Identify Challenges:** What are the challenges the team faces in the decision-making process?
2. **Impact Analysis:** What is the impact of these challenges on decision quality and employee satisfaction?
3. **Develop Strategies to Enhance Participation:** What strategies will we use to enhance employee participation in decision-making?
4. **Implement Strategies:** How will we apply these strategies in daily work?
5. **Monitor Progress:** How will we evaluate the impact of the strategies and make necessary adjustments?

Exercise: Workshop to Enhance Group Decision-Making

Gather your team for a workshop to identify potential challenges and develop strategies to enhance participation in decision-making. Use brainstorming sessions to analyze the impact and develop detailed plans for each team.

Inspiring Quotes

"Participation is the secret to success in the modern work environment." - Anonymous

"Collective decision-making is the result of multiple minds and diverse experiences." - Anonymous

Discussion Questions

1. How can your team enhance participation in the decision-making process?
2. What strategies can be used to foster effective participation?
3. How can you balance the speed of decision-making with the quality resulting from participation?

Chapter Eleven: Developing a Collaborative Work Environment

Story: Enhancing Collaboration at Tech Excel
After achieving significant successes by improving various operations, Adam realized that the next step to ensure sustained success was to develop a collaborative work environment. He knew that effective collaboration between teams and individuals could lead to higher levels of creativity and efficiency.

The Challenge: Enhancing Team Collaboration
At one of the monthly meetings, Adam noticed that some teams were working in silos, leading to a lack of communication and collaboration between different departments. The goal was to break down these barriers and foster a collaborative work environment that contributes to achieving common goals.

The Importance of Collaboration in the Workplace
Adam began by explaining the importance of collaboration in the workplace. He pointed out that collaborative work enhances the exchange of ideas and experiences, contributing to faster and more effective problem-solving. Additionally, collaboration boosts team spirit and increases job satisfaction.

"Welcome to our monthly meeting. There is an important issue I would like to discuss today. I have noticed that some teams are working in isolation, which has led to a lack of communication and collaboration between different departments. Our goal is to break down these barriers and foster a collaborative work environment that contributes to achieving common goals."

Sarah: "Yes, I have noticed this too in the customer service department. Some of the challenges we face could be better resolved if we communicated with other teams, especially the tech department."

Kareem: "I believe that inter-departmental collaboration will help improve our marketing strategies. If we have a better understanding of the challenges faced by the tech or customer service departments, we can direct our efforts more effectively."

Adam: "Exactly. Collaborative work enhances the exchange of ideas and experiences, contributing to faster and more effective problem-solving. Additionally, collaboration boosts team spirit and increases job satisfaction. Let's discuss how to enhance this collaboration."

Youssef: "What if we organized regular meetings between different departments to discuss joint projects and the challenges we face? These meetings could be an opportunity to exchange ideas and work on common solutions."

Leila: "Good idea. I also think we can use project management tools that allow all teams to see the progress and challenges of other departments."

Hala: "Yes, and we could also organize interactive training workshops that bring together employees from different departments to work together on solving specific problems. This would help build stronger relationships between teams and enhance collaboration."

Adam: "Great, let's outline some practical steps to implement these ideas. Youssef, can you organize the regular inter-departmental meetings?"

Youssef: "Sure, I'll start by organizing an initial meeting next week, and we'll see how we can establish this system regularly."

Leila: "I'll review the available project management tools and determine which ones are most suitable for our company."

Hala: "And I'll work on organizing the first interactive training workshop that brings together employees from different departments. We can start with a small workshop and then gradually expand."

Adam: "Excellent. Let's start implementing these ideas and follow up on the progress in our next meeting. Thank you all for your enthusiasm and cooperation. Together, we can achieve a more collaborative and effective work environment."

Initial Interdepartmental Meeting:

Youssef: "Hello everyone, thank you for coming today. As you know, we are here to kick off a system of regular interdepartmental meetings to enhance collaboration and communication. This is our first session, and I'd like to discuss some key points and determine how we can work together more effectively."

Sarah: "I think this is a great idea, Youssef. In the customer service department, we face some challenges that I believe we could address better if we collaborate with other departments."

Kareem: "Yes, and from our side in marketing, we need a better understanding of the challenges faced by the technology and customer service departments so that we can direct our efforts more precisely."

Leila: "I agree with that. In finance, it's important for us to understand how decisions made by other departments impact our budgets and resource allocation."

Youssef: "Excellent. Let's start by setting some core objectives for these meetings. I believe the first goal should be to identify the common challenges we face and work on collective solutions."

Hala: "Good idea. We can also allocate part of the meeting to sharing updates on current projects in each department, which will help us stay informed and see how we can support each other."

Nadia: "I think using project management tools could help with this. We can use a platform that allows us to share updates, track progress, and monitor challenges."

Youssef: "Definitely, we'll need to decide on the tools we'll use. I believe Leila is already reviewing available tools and will provide recommendations at our next meeting."

Leila: "Certainly."

Youssef: "Great. Let's now discuss how to organize these meetings. What would be an appropriate frequency? Do you prefer meeting weekly or bi-weekly?"

Sarah: "I think meeting bi-weekly would be suitable. This will give us enough time to work on the tasks and challenges we discuss in the meetings."

Kareem: "Agreed. Bi-weekly seems appropriate, and we can always adjust the schedule as needed."

Youssef: "Alright, then we'll start with meetings every two weeks. We'll use these meetings as an opportunity to discuss challenges, share updates, and work together on solutions. Are there any other suggestions before we wrap up?"

Hala: "I don't think so. I believe we're on the right track. Thank you for organizing this, Youssef."

Youssef: "Thank you all for attending and participating. Let's make these meetings effective and achieve better collaboration. We'll meet again in two weeks. Thank you!"

Workshop: Enhancing Interdepartmental Collaboration

Preparation and Setup:
- **Selecting Participants:** Choose a few employees from each department (Marketing, Customer Service, Finance, Technology, Human Resources) to attend the first workshop.

- **Defining Objectives:** The main goal is to enhance collaboration and exchange ideas and experiences to solve common problems.
- **Tools and Materials:** Prepare training materials and necessary tools (e.g., worksheets, brainstorming tools, interactive techniques).

Starting the Workshop:

Hala: "Welcome everyone to our first training workshop on enhancing interdepartmental collaboration. I'm glad to see you all here today. Our goal is to work together to enhance collaboration and exchange ideas and experiences between different departments."

Opening Session:

Adam: "Thank you, Hala. I want to start by explaining why we consider this workshop important. Collaboration between departments is not just a good idea; it is essential for achieving our common goals more effectively. Let's begin with a quick introduction session."

Session 1: Team Building and Introduction

- **Introduction Activity:** Participants are divided into small teams, where each member gets to know the others and shares information about their role and daily challenges.
- **Role Exchange:** Each participant explains their tasks and responsibilities to others in the team.

Youssef: "It's helpful to understand our colleagues' roles and responsibilities. This helps us appreciate the challenges each department faces and how we can support each other."

Session 2: Brainstorming for Problem-Solving

- **Identifying Common Problems:** A set of challenges faced by the company is identified, which requires joint solutions.
- **Brainstorming Sessions:** Teams brainstorm to propose creative solutions to these challenges.
- **Presenting Results:** Each team presents their results and suggestions to the other teams.

Sarah: "We've noticed that some challenges we face in customer service can be better solved if we collaborate with the technology department to improve our tools."

Session 3: Developing Collaboration Strategies

- **Creating Collaboration Plans:** Develop practical plans to enhance collaboration between departments, including setting up regular communication methods and information exchange.
- **Defining Responsibilities:** Assign roles and responsibilities for each department in implementing the collaboration plans.

Kareem: "It's good to establish clear points of contact between different departments to ensure smooth information flow."

Closing Session: Evaluation and Follow-Up

- **Evaluation:** The workshop is evaluated by participants to review what has been learned and how future workshops can be improved.
- **Follow-Up:** Determine follow-up steps to ensure effective implementation of collaboration plans.

Hala: "Thank you all for your active participation. We will collect your feedback to improve future workshops and expand them to include more employees."

Adam: "This workshop was an important first step toward enhancing collaboration between our departments. Let's continue to work together to achieve our common goals."

Strategies for Developing a Collaborative Work Environment

1. **Encourage Open and Honest Communication:**
   - Organize regular meetings between teams to discuss joint projects and challenges.
   - Utilize technological tools that facilitate instant and direct communication among employees.
2. **Foster Team Spirit:**
   - Organize team-building activities that strengthen bonds between employees.
   - Encourage employees to participate in social events and external activities.
3. **Develop Collaborative Workspaces:**
   - Design open workspaces that allow employees to interact easily.

- Provide common areas for informal meetings and idea exchanges.
4. **Provide Collaboration Skills Training:**
    - Offer training programs focused on effective communication and teamwork skills.
    - Enhance collaborative leadership skills that promote idea sharing and respect for diverse perspectives.
5. **Encourage Joint Projects:**
    - Promote teamwork on joint projects that combine different expertise.
    - Provide rewards and incentives for teams that achieve success in collaborative projects.

Success Stories from Enhancing Collaboration in the Company

Success Story of the Marketing and Sales Team:

In a new product launch project, the marketing team worked closely with the sales team. Joint brainstorming sessions and continuous idea exchanges were organized. Thanks to this collaboration, a successful marketing campaign was developed, leading to a significant increase in sales in a short period.

Improving Internal Processes:

The HR team collaborated with the IT team to develop a new performance management system. Thanks to the continuous cooperation and coordination between the two teams, the system was successfully implemented, leading to improved performance evaluation processes and increased transparency in assessments.

Lessons Learned:

1. **The Importance of Collaboration in the Workplace:**
   - Collaboration enhances idea sharing and creativity, and increases problem-solving efficiency.
   - A collaborative work environment contributes to higher employee satisfaction and fosters team spirit.
2. **Effective Strategies for Developing a Collaborative Work Environment:**
   - Encouraging open and honest communication helps build bridges of cooperation between teams.
   - Organizing team-building activities and developing collaborative workspaces strengthens employee bonds.
   - Providing training in collaboration skills enhances the effectiveness of teamwork.
3. **Success Stories Demonstrating the Effectiveness of Collaboration:**
   - Joint efforts between marketing and sales teams led to a successful marketing campaign and increased sales.
   - Improving internal processes through collaboration between HR and IT.

By fostering a collaborative work environment, Adam and his team at "Tech Excel" achieved higher levels of creativity and efficiency. This step was crucial in enhancing the company's culture and increasing employee satisfaction, underscoring that effective collaboration is key to success in the modern workplace.

Tools and Practical Exercises to Enhance Team Collaboration

Tool: Collaborative Team Building Model

1. **Setting Common Goals:**
   - What are the main goals that each team is striving to achieve?
   - How can these goals be integrated to achieve mutual success?
2. **Establishing Effective Communication Channels:**
   - What tools and technologies can be used to improve communication between teams?
   - How can access to information and resources be facilitated across departments?
3. **Encouraging Idea Sharing:**
   - How can an environment be created that encourages employees to freely share their ideas?
   - What are the ways to recognize and reward new ideas?
4. **Strengthening Teamwork:**
   - What activities and exercises can be organized to enhance team spirit?
   - How can tasks be allocated in a way that fosters collaboration and leverages the skills of all members?
5. **Monitoring and Evaluating Progress:**
   - What criteria can be used to measure the level of collaboration between teams?

- How can constructive feedback be provided to improve collaborative processes?

Exercise: Workshop to Enhance Collaboration

Objective: To strengthen collaboration and idea-sharing among employees from different departments.

1. **Icebreaker Activity:**
    - Divide participants into mixed teams.
    - Have each member introduce themselves and share information about their role and daily challenges.
2. **Brainstorming Session:**
    - Identify a common problem or challenge that needs solving.
    - Have the teams work together to propose creative solutions.
3. **Presenting Results:**
    - Allow each team to present their ideas and suggestions to the rest of the participants.
    - Discuss how these ideas can be practically implemented.
4. **Creating Collaboration Plans:**
    - Have teams develop practical plans to enhance collaboration between departments.
    - Define the roles and responsibilities of each department in implementing these plans.

Inspirational Quotes

"Collaboration is the ability to work together toward a common vision. It is the fuel that allows individuals to achieve extraordinary results." - Andrew Carnegie

"Teamwork is the key to success, and the more we collaborate, the stronger we become." - Henry Ford

"Collaboration is what brings us together, and teamwork is what makes us succeed." - Steve Jobs

---

Discussion Questions

1. How can we enhance collaboration between teams in our company?
2. What challenges do we face in collaboration between different departments, and how can we overcome them?
3. How can we improve the tools and methods of communication between departments?
4. What strategies can we use to strengthen team spirit among employees?
5. How can our future projects benefit from team collaboration?

Chapter 12: Periodic Performance Evaluation

Story: Tech Excel's Experience with Performance Evaluation

Adam knew that maintaining the success that Tech Excel had achieved required a strong mechanism for periodic performance evaluation. He wanted to ensure that every employee felt valued and guided, and that they were aware of their performance levels and future goals.

The Challenge: Evaluating Performance Effectively and Fairly

At the beginning, Adam and the leadership team faced a challenge in designing a performance evaluation system that was both fair and effective. Some employees felt that previous evaluations were neither transparent nor fair, which affected their satisfaction and performance. Therefore, it was necessary to restructure the process to make it more transparent and objective.

Adam: "Hello everyone. Thank you for being here today. We have a significant challenge ahead of us, which is redesigning the performance evaluation system to be more transparent and fair. I've received feedback from several employees that the current system lacks transparency and objectivity, which negatively impacts their satisfaction and performance."

Leila: "Yes, I've heard that too from some colleagues in the Finance department. They feel that the evaluations aren't based on clear criteria, and this causes a lot of frustration."

Hala: "In the Customer Service department, there's a similar feeling. We need a system that clearly outlines what's expected of everyone and how they can continuously improve their performance."

Kareem: "I think the first step we need to take is to establish clear and objective criteria for performance evaluation. Employees need to know what goals they need to achieve and how they will be evaluated."

Youssef: "I agree with you, Kareem. It's also important that there is continuous communication between supervisors and employees. The evaluation should be an ongoing process, not just an annual event."

Adam: "Exactly. Let's start by identifying some basic criteria that we need in the new system. What factors do we consider essential for a fair performance evaluation?"

Sarah: "I believe that individual performance should be evaluated based on specific criteria such as goal achievement, work quality, and adherence to deadlines."

Leila: "We should also consider interpersonal skills, such as the ability to work in a team, initiative, and problem-solving abilities."

Kareem: "And let's not forget the importance of continuous learning and development. There could be a component in the evaluation that depends on how much an employee invests in developing their skills."

Adam: "Good, so we have several basic criteria: individual performance, interpersonal skills, and continuous learning and development. Now, let's think about how to make these criteria transparent for everyone. How about creating a comprehensive guide that explains how each criterion will be evaluated?"

Youssef: "Great idea. The guide could include examples of behaviors and actions that demonstrate achieving these criteria."

Sarah: "We could also organize training workshops for supervisors and employees to explain the new system and how to use it effectively."

Adam: "Excellent. Let's set up an action plan to implement this system. Leila, can you work on drafting the first version of the guide?"

Leila: "Of course, I'll start on it right away."

Youssef: "I'll work on organizing the training workshops. We can start the first workshop next week."

Adam: "Great. Thank you all for the fantastic ideas. I'm confident that this new system will make the performance evaluation process more fair and transparent, which will increase employee satisfaction and motivation."

Everyone: "Thank you, Adam."

The Importance of Regular Performance Evaluation

The importance of regular performance evaluation cannot be overstated. It's not just about measuring performance, but also about fostering personal and professional growth for employees. Regular evaluations help to:

- Identify employees' strengths and weaknesses.
- Provide constructive feedback to improve performance.
- Set future goals and guide career paths.
- Motivate employees by recognizing their achievements and offering appropriate rewards.

Workshop: Designing a Performance Evaluation System

Youssef: "Hello everyone. Thank you for attending today's first workshop on the new performance evaluation system. Our goal today is to explain the new system and how to use it effectively to ensure transparency and fairness in performance evaluations. Let's start by outlining the key criteria we'll be using in the evaluation."

Leila: "The key criteria we've identified include: individual performance, interpersonal skills, and continuous learning and development. Each criterion will be evaluated based on a set of specific behaviors and actions."

Sarah: "Let's break down each criterion and explain how it will be assessed. For individual performance, we'll look at goal achievement, work quality, and meeting deadlines. Employees can submit monthly or quarterly reports highlighting their accomplishments and goals achieved."

Kareem: "For interpersonal skills, we'll assess the ability to work in a team, initiative, and problem-solving abilities. Supervisors can provide examples of specific behaviors they've observed throughout the year."

Youssef: "Continuous learning and development will be based on the employee's investment in skill development. Employees can present certificates of training courses they've attended or new projects they've worked on to enhance their skills."

Adam: "Alright, let's move on to a practical activity. I'll divide you into small groups, and each group will work on creating practical examples of how to apply these criteria in performance evaluations."

(The participants are divided into small groups, and each group begins working on creating practical examples.)

Youssef (after 20 minutes): "Let's hear what the teams have come up with. Sara's team, could you start?"

Sarah: "Certainly. For the individual performance criterion, we determined that goal achievement can be evaluated based on Key Performance Indicators (KPIs) that were agreed upon at the beginning of the year. For example, in customer service, a KPI could be the customer satisfaction rate."

Leila: "Our team suggested that teamwork skills could be assessed through peer feedback and the employee's participation in team projects. Positive behaviors might include active participation in meetings and offering assistance to colleagues."

Kareem: "Our team focused on continuous learning and development. We proposed that employees be required to submit reports on training courses they've attended or certifications they've earned. Development can also be assessed through innovative projects they're working on."

Youssef: "Excellent! Thank you all for the great ideas. Now, let's discuss how we can ensure transparency in the evaluation process. Leila, do you have some ideas?"

Leila: "Yes, we can prepare a comprehensive guide that outlines how each criterion is evaluated, along with specific examples. We could also organize regular review sessions with employees to ensure they understand the criteria and how they can improve their performance."

Adam: "I think it's also important to maintain continuous communication between supervisors and employees. We could hold semi-annual meetings to discuss performance progress and provide constructive feedback."

Youssef: "Exactly. We'll also work on creating an online platform where employees can track their progress and upload documents related to their evaluations."

Hala: "Are there any other questions or suggestions?"

Participant: "I think regular training sessions would help us better understand the system and ensure its effective implementation."

Youssef: "Great idea. We'll organize regular training workshops to clarify the system and help everyone use it effectively."

Adam: "Thank you all for your active participation. Let's work together to ensure the success of this system and create a fair and transparent work environment."

Strategies for Regular Performance Evaluation
1. Establish Clear Evaluation Criteria:
- Define specific performance criteria for each role, including quantitative and qualitative goals.
- Ensure that the criteria are understood and accepted by all employees.

2. Comprehensive 360-Degree Evaluation:
- Collect feedback from various colleagues, managers, and clients to provide a comprehensive view of the employee's performance.
- Use technological tools to facilitate the collection and analysis of feedback.

3. Set Regular Evaluation Periods:
- Conduct semi-annual and annual evaluations to ensure continuous performance monitoring.
- Organize regular review sessions to discuss progress and challenges.

4. Provide Constructive and Immediate Feedback:
- Offer constructive feedback to help employees improve their performance.

- o Provide feedback immediately after significant events to maintain timeliness and objectivity.

5. Develop Personal Growth Plans:
- o Work with each employee to develop a personal growth plan that outlines goals and the training needed to improve performance.
- o Provide support and resources to achieve these goals.

Success Stories from Implementing the New Performance Evaluation System

Sara's Success Story:

Sara, a technical support employee at "Tech Excel," was feeling dissatisfied due to a lack of guidance and recognition. After implementing the new evaluation system, she received constructive feedback on her strengths and areas for improvement. A training plan was developed to enhance her technical skills. Thanks to these efforts, Sara's performance improved significantly, her job satisfaction increased, and she received a promotion in recognition of her efforts.

Improving Overall Company Performance:

Through regular evaluations, the leadership team discovered that some processes needed improvement. Feedback from employees was collected to identify areas for enhancement. This led to the development of new procedures that increased work efficiency and reduced errors, contributing to improved overall company performance and increased customer satisfaction.

Lessons Learned:
1. **Importance of Regular Performance Evaluation:**
   - Regular evaluations enhance employees' personal and professional growth.
   - Helps in identifying strengths and weaknesses and providing the appropriate support to improve performance.
2. **Effective Performance Evaluation Strategies:**
   - Establishing clear and comprehensive evaluation criteria ensures fairness and transparency.
   - Using 360-degree evaluations provides a complete picture of employee performance.
   - Providing constructive and timely feedback improves the timing and effectiveness of evaluations.
3. **Success Stories Highlighting the Effectiveness of Regular Evaluations:**
   - Improving employee performance and job satisfaction through regular evaluations and constructive feedback.
   - Developing company processes and increasing efficiency through regular feedback collection and analysis.

By implementing a regular performance evaluation system, Adam and his team at "Tech Excel" were able to enhance employee performance and increase job satisfaction. This step was crucial in advancing the company's growth and developing its competitive capabilities, confirming that regular evaluations are not just a measurement tool but a means for continuous development and motivation.

Tools and Practical Exercises
Tool: Periodic Performance Evaluation System

1. **Defining Performance Criteria:**
   - What are the essential criteria that should be used to evaluate employee performance?
   - How can these criteria be established so that they are clear and understandable to all employees?
2. **Comprehensive 360-Degree Evaluation:**
   - What are the various sources from which feedback can be gathered to provide a comprehensive evaluation?
   - How can technology be used to facilitate the process of collecting and analyzing feedback?
3. **Setting Regular Evaluation Periods:**
   - How often should evaluations be conducted to ensure continuous performance monitoring?
   - What are the best times during the year to conduct these evaluations?
4. **Providing Constructive and Immediate Feedback:**
   - How can feedback be delivered in a constructive manner that helps employees improve their performance?
   - What is the best way to provide feedback immediately after key events to maintain timing and objectivity?
5. **Developing Personal Growth Plans:**
   - How can you work with each employee to develop a personal growth plan that outlines the goals and training needed to improve performance?

- What resources and support can be provided to achieve these goals?

Exercise: Workshop for Designing a Performance Evaluation System

Goal: Create a transparent and fair performance evaluation system that enhances employee satisfaction and improves the overall performance of the company.

Steps:

1. **Gather the Team:** Bring your team together in a workshop to identify the key performance criteria for each job in the company.
2. **Define Criteria:** Establish clear performance criteria that include quantitative and qualitative goals, interpersonal skills, and continuous learning and development.
3. **Prepare a Guide:** Develop a comprehensive guide that explains how each criterion will be evaluated, with examples of the required behaviors and actions.
4. **Organize Training Workshops:** Conduct training workshops for supervisors and employees to explain the new system and how to use it effectively.
5. **Provide Feedback:** Conduct a practical exercise on how to give constructive and immediate feedback, with real-life examples.

Inspirational Quotes

"Periodic evaluation is not just a tool for measurement but a means for continuous development and motivation." - John C. Maxwell

"Fair evaluation fosters trust and satisfaction among employees and drives them to achieve their best." - Peter Drucker

---

Discussion Questions

1. How can periodic evaluation affect employee satisfaction and performance?
2. What are the essential criteria that should be included in the performance evaluation process?
3. How can we ensure transparency and fairness in the performance evaluation system?
4. What benefits can employees and the company gain from implementing a comprehensive and regular performance evaluation system?
5. How can immediate and constructive feedback improve employee performance and contribute to their professional growth?

Chapter Thirteen: Sustainability and Social Responsibility

With the company's increasing success and continuous growth, Adam and his team realized the importance of thinking more deeply about the future. The goal was not only to achieve financial success but also to leave a positive impact on society and the environment. Therefore, they decided to adopt strategies aimed at enhancing the company's sustainability and social responsibility.

A New Vision for Sustainability

Adam held an extensive meeting with the leadership team to discuss how to integrate sustainability into the company's strategic vision. All key managers, along with some employees, attended the meeting.

"Sustainability is not just a moral duty; it's also an opportunity to foster innovation and create long-term value for the company and society," Adam began the meeting.

Adam: "Hello everyone, thank you for joining us today. As you know, we're here to discuss how to integrate sustainability into our strategic vision. Sustainability is not just a moral duty; it's also an opportunity to foster innovation and create long-term value for the company and society."

Leila: "I agree with you, Adam. Sustainability can help us reduce costs in the long run, especially if we focus on resource and energy efficiency."

Hala: "And I believe customers appreciate companies that care about sustainability. It can enhance customer loyalty and trust."

Kareem: "But how do we start? What are the first steps we need to take to integrate sustainability into our daily operations?"

Adam: "First, we need to identify the key areas of focus. These could be improving energy efficiency, reducing waste, and using renewable resources. What do you all think?"

Sarah: "I think improving energy efficiency should be a top priority. We could start by assessing energy consumption in each department and identifying actions we can take to reduce it."

Youssef: "We could also invest in green technology, like using energy-efficient devices and AI applications to manage resources more efficiently."

Leila: "Additionally, we could consider recycling waste and turning it into resources. This could reduce waste disposal costs and create new opportunities for utilization."

Adam: "Great, let's set some short-term and long-term goals. For example, a short-term goal could be reducing energy consumption by 10% within the next year, while a long-term goal could be transitioning the company to 100% renewable energy sources within five years."

Hala: "We should also ensure that employees are engaged in these initiatives. We can organize awareness workshops and internal campaigns to encourage active participation."

Kareem: "And we should consider our supply chain as well. We can choose suppliers who adhere to sustainability standards to ensure that every stage of our production aligns with our vision."

Sarah: "Let's create a sustainability committee with representatives from each department. This committee would be responsible for tracking the implementation of initiatives and providing regular progress reports."

Adam: "Great idea, Sara. Let's decide who will be on this committee and hold an initial meeting next week. Any other suggestions?"

Youssef: "I also suggest collaborating with NGOs or educational institutions that can provide advice and assistance in implementing sustainability projects."

Leila: "We could also offer incentives to employees who contribute new ideas to achieve our sustainability goals."

Adam: "Excellent, it looks like we have a solid action plan. I'll document these points and share them with you in a follow-up meeting later today. Thank you all for your active participation. Together, we can achieve a lot."

Everyone: "Thank you, Adam."

Setting Sustainability Goals

The meeting began with a brainstorming session to set the main sustainability goals. Leila led the session, where the team prioritized sustainability initiatives encompassing environmental and social aspects.

Leila: "Welcome, everyone, and thank you for joining. As you know, we are here today to identify the sustainability priorities that will guide our strategic vision. Let's start with a brainstorming session to determine the main sustainability goals, covering both environmental and social aspects. We'll begin by identifying the areas we believe are most important for our company and community. Does anyone have any initial suggestions?"

Kareem: "I think improving energy efficiency should be at the top of our priorities. We could start by assessing energy consumption across departments and work on reducing waste."

Sarah: "I agree with Kareem. Additionally, we could focus on waste reduction by enhancing recycling programs and using biodegradable materials."

Hala: "On the social side, we could focus on improving the work environment and enhancing employee well-being. This could include mental health programs and professional training and development."

Youssef: "We shouldn't forget the role of technology in achieving sustainability. We could invest in technological solutions that reduce energy consumption and increase operational efficiency."

Adam: "What about engaging with the local community? We could launch initiatives to support education and training in technology and environmental fields."

Leila: "Excellent. We now have several areas we want to focus on: energy efficiency, waste reduction, employee well-being, technology investment, and community support. Let's set specific goals for each area. For example, regarding energy efficiency, what goals do we want to achieve over the next year?"

Kareem: "We could start by reducing energy consumption by 15% over the next year by using more efficient devices and replacing outdated systems."

Sarah: "In terms of waste reduction, our goal could be to recycle 50% of the company's waste by the end of the year."

Hala: "For employee well-being, we could conduct regular surveys to measure employee satisfaction and offer training and educational programs that meet their needs."

Youssef: "In the technology area, we could allocate part of the R&D budget to develop sustainable technological solutions, such as smart energy management systems."

Adam: "And for community support, we could organize training workshops in collaboration with local schools and universities, and offer scholarships in technology and environmental fields."

Leila: "Great. Let's summarize what we've reached:

1. **Energy Efficiency:** Reduce energy consumption by 15% over the next year.
2. **Waste Reduction:** Recycle 50% of the company's waste by the end of the year.
3. **Employee Well-being:** Conduct regular surveys and provide training and educational programs.
4. **Investment in Technology:** Allocate a budget for R&D to develop sustainable technological solutions.
5. **Support for the Local Community:** Organize training workshops and provide scholarships."

Adam: "Thank you, Leila, for leading this productive session. Now we have clear goals to work on. I'll follow up with each department to ensure these goals are achieved. Are there any suggestions or comments before we wrap up the meeting?"

Participant: "I think we have a good plan. Let's get to work on implementing it."

Leila: "We need to be ambitious yet realistic at the same time. These goals will help us contribute to a more sustainable future. Thank you all for your participation. Let's work together to achieve these goals and make our company more sustainable."

Everyone: "Thank you, Leila."

Strategic Partnerships

Developing Partnerships with NGOs
The team decided to develop strategic partnerships with NGOs and other companies to strengthen sustainability initiatives. Kareem reached out to several environmental organizations for advice and collaboration.

Implementation and Follow-up

Execution and Follow-up Plans
The teams began implementing the established sustainability plans. Youssef led a planning session to implement eco-friendly technologies in production processes, while Sarah led a session to develop training programs focused on sustainability and social responsibility.

- **Technology Team:** Develop eco-friendly production technologies, improve energy efficiency.
- **Human Resources Team:** Organize training programs on sustainability, enhance diversity and inclusion.
- **Finance Team:** Budget for green initiatives, assess the financial feasibility of sustainability investments.

"We need to be committed to monitoring the implementation of our plans and adjusting them as needed to ensure we achieve our goals," said Adam.

Tools and Practical Exercises
Tool: Sustainability Plan Template

1. **Set Objectives:** What are the main sustainability goals you want to achieve?
2. **Develop Strategies:** What strategies will you use to achieve these goals?
3. **Implement Plans:** What practical steps are needed to implement these strategies?
4. **Monitor Progress:** How will progress be monitored and results evaluated?
5. **Continuous Adjustments:** What mechanisms will you use to adapt to challenges and adjust plans as needed?

Exercise: Sustainability Workshop

Gather your team in a workshop to identify and develop sustainability plans. Use brainstorming sessions and collaborative planning to create actionable strategies and monitor progress.

Inspirational Quotes

"Sustainability is not just about doing what is right; it is also a path to achieving lasting success." - Paul Polman

"Every small step towards sustainability contributes to creating a better future." - Jacqueline Augustin

---

Discussion Questions

1. How can we foster a culture of sustainability in our company?
2. What challenges might we face in implementing sustainability plans, and how can we overcome them?
3. How can strategic partnerships contribute to achieving sustainability goals?

Chapter Fourteen: Lessons Learned and Future Vision

Reviewing the Journey

Summarizing Challenges and Successes

After several years of hard work and ongoing challenges, Adam and his team gathered to assess the journey they had undertaken. The company had undergone many transformations, starting with improved communication and strategic planning, followed by the development of organizational capabilities and the implementation of sustainability initiatives.

"It has been a journey full of challenges, but we have achieved a lot thanks to the team's collaboration and our commitment to our vision," Adam said proudly.

Lessons Learned

Learning from Experiences

The team discussed the key lessons they had learned along the way:

1. **The Importance of Effective Communication:** Everyone emphasized that open and transparent communication was essential to achieving common goals.
2. **Adaptability to Change:** Youssef pointed out that the ability to quickly adapt to challenges and changes was key to their success.

3. **Investment in Training:** Sarah emphasized that continuous training and skill development had a significant impact on the team's performance.
4. **Commitment to Sustainability:** Leila spoke about how sustainability was not just a social responsibility but also an opportunity to create long-term value.

Future Vision

Planning for the Future

After reviewing the achievements and lessons learned, the team discussed the company's future steps. They all agreed to continue their commitment to innovation and continuous development.

"The future is full of opportunities, and we must be ready to seize them. We will continue to focus on improving our products and services while enhancing our sustainability and social responsibility," Adam said.

Practical Tools and Exercises
Tool: Performance Evaluation Model
1. **Identify Achieved Goals:** Review the goals that were achieved during the previous period.
2. **Gap Analysis:** Identify the gaps between the achieved goals and the planned goals.
3. **Develop Improvement Plans:** Create plans to improve performance and close the gaps.
4. **Determine Required Resources:** Identify the resources needed to implement the improvement plans.
5. **Regular Review:** Set a schedule for regular performance reviews.

Exercise: Performance Evaluation Session
Gather your team for a performance evaluation session and review the achieved goals. Use the Performance Evaluation Model to identify successes and challenges and to develop plans for continuous improvement.

Inspirational Quotes
"Continuous learning is the key to success in a rapidly changing world." - John C. Maxwell
"Vision without execution is a dream; execution without vision is a nightmare." - Thomas Edison

---

Discussion Questions
1. How can we continue to improve communication within the team?
2. What steps can we take to enhance sustainability in all aspects of our work?
3. How can we ensure commitment to our vision and future goals?

Conclusion

As we reach the end of this book, it becomes evident that the path to progress is not without challenges and hardships. However, by committing to continuous learning and adapting to changes, we find ourselves equipped with the necessary tools to face any challenge that comes our way. We have learned from past experiences that open communication, investment in innovation, and a commitment to sustainability are the keys to success in a world that demands us to look forward with confidence and faith in our ability to make positive change.

Each lesson and piece of advice in this book should be seen as a step toward progress and development. We encourage you to view them as a guide on your personal and professional journey. The future awaits us with its opportunities and challenges, and if we can overcome obstacles and achieve a balance between innovation and sustainability, we will be on the right path to building a better world for everyone.